BELT &

C000253687

Cover and Frontispiece:
Young Toby flanked by Father and Mother.

BELT &
BUCKLE

Toby Dyer

Illustrations by Gill Younger

EX LIBRIS PRESS

First published in 1993 by
EX LIBRIS PRESS
1 The Shambles
Bradford on Avon
Wiltshire

Typeset in 10 point Century Schoolbook

Design and Typesetting by Ex Libris Press

Cover printed by Shires Press, Trowbridge
Printed and bound in Britain by
Cromwell Press Ltd., Broughton Gifford, Wiltshire

ISBN 0 978578 54 8

Acknowledgements
To Sarah, whose second finger made typing a new age technology;
and Nigel and Pauline for insisting that paragraphs were not sky-
divers' perfomance charts.

CONTENTS

About the author

Toby Dyer was born and raised in the West Country, the only son of an agricultural worker and his wife who had, due to advancing years, given up hope of any children.

His early years were pretty itinerant as he moved from tied cottage to tied cottage and school to school following his Father's employment. He eventually left school at fifteen with no qualifications and, after working for a time in agriculture, joined his County Regiment where he served for five years without great distinction, being described by his commanding officer as 'a quick-witted young soldier with a sense of adventure but with too restless and sceptical a temperament for the British Army!'

He left the Army to become an Inspector with the RSPCA, serving for three and a half years in London's East End and then, by complete contrast, in the sleepy Wiltshire market town of Devizes. It was in Wiltshire that the chance acquisition of some country 'bygones' led to him building up a collection of over 1200 items, described by many informed sources as 'the finest and best researched collection of its type in private hands.'

This led to the establishment of a Country Life Museum at Cricket St. Thomas near Chard. However, after ten years, redevelopment meant the site was required for other purposes, and the collection was sold at auction in 1990. Springing from this, Toby Dyer published four titles in the Shire Album series: *Shepherding Tools and Customs*, *Dairying Bygones*, *Trapping and Poaching* and *The Country Animal Doctor*.

Today he rents an ancient ham-stone farmhouse with Sarah, young son Barnaby and a sundry throng of animals at the end of a multi-rutted mud track in south Somerset and scratches a meagre living as a self-employed handyman.

1.
Bombers, Birthrights and Dancing Pigs

THE JUNKERS BOMBERS droning overhead were not Junkers bombers. Wellingtons perhaps, or possibly Lancasters. Without doubt something heavy and menacing, but certainly nothing Mr Goering would have authorised. In my Father's mind however, Junkers they most certainly were. A swarming black cloud, heading north to unleash Armageddon once more upon the unfortunate city of Bristol.

He brooded for scarce a moment upon the injustice of German High Command disrupting his life by pencilling in their bomber flight path over Yeovil, before summoning my Mother with a harsh cry of 'Gwen'. Mother, slight, and sparrow-shouldered, scampered in from the kitchen, where she had been engaged in an unequal struggle to change the wick in the paraffin stove. She had taken the situation fully on board, even before Father, irately jabbing an accusing finger towards the living room ceiling, snarled "Bloody Krauts again, do they never leave off?"

They both realized the expedient thing to do next, and pausing only to gather up a couple of cushions, a candle and a newspaper, they hastened to the cupboard under the stairs.

Built as part of an old agricultural worker's cottage, it formed an integral part of the accommodation, used as a store for homemade preserves and wines, and often referred to as the 'glory hole'. Although still cramped, it was considerably more commodious than its counterpart in a more modern house.

Once ensconced, Father with both cushions and the newspaper, and Mother with the candle, they resigned themselves to the long wait. It was common knowledge that having attacked their target the Germans would return along their flight path. Should any not have discharged their bombs, they would quite probably, if harrassed by our own fighters, shed their payload at random across the countryside, increasing their own speed and manoeuvrability to effect escape. And so it was, armed with this knowledge, that the two of

7

them huddled in their dingy lair – Father with all the creature comforts, bristling indignation, Mother clutching candle, fearful and lachrymose.

"Dun't bide 'n' snivel," growled Father peevishly. "Tis bad enough bein' stuck in these yere 'ole wi'out you blubbin' yer eye!"

It was as close as his nature would allow him to issuing soft words of comfort, particularly as his fascination with the newspaper had become quickly exhausted. The sports page was a bit thin in wartime, anyhow he'd read it earlier. Even the humour of Pip, Squeak and Wilfred sailed well over *his* head. He grunted, folded the newspaper in four and wedged it between the back of his head and the wall.

His mind drifted to Bristol. The poor unfortunates being subjected to hell on earth, death being dealt by a random hand in the sky, never knowing if the next one 'had your name on it'; the city centre reduced to smouldering rubble. Ah the obscenities of war!

He inwardly hoped against hope that their torment would be brief, for wasn't he just dying for a cup of tea. "Was it worth risking a sortie into the kitchen to make one?" he pondered. Reluctantly he decided against it, as it meant disturbing himself to facilitate Mother's exit. His mind became re-aligned to the injustice of it all. Troops and airmen cornering all the kudos.

"What about those in reserved occupations?" he mused rhetorically, "We're all doing our bit." He'd bet old Montgommery wouldn't have to be up at 5.30 in the morning to milk the bloody cows!

His mind drifted slowly through from indignation to self pity, to boredom, to drowsy indifference, to amour. Yes, amour. There was little doubt that disturbing feelings were abroad in his recumbent body, and all their directional indicators were pointing, like windspeed arrows on a weather chart, towards his loins. The close proximity of a warm female body, even if it was only that of his own wife, pressed, sardine-like in a confined space, was beginning to stimulate a carnal need.

The logistics of arranging two bodies in a coital position in the cramped confines experienced here, are best left to the fertile imaginations of those who have, at some time, owned a B.M.C. Mini. But I do have it on first hand information, collected piecemeal over the years, that arrange it they somehow did.

Perhaps it would be as well at this juncture to explain, that for all his fiercely held political dogma, Father was essentially a simple man of the soil. True, he had served for twelve years as a stoker in

Father with both cushions and the newspaper.

His Majesty's Navy, distinguishing himself with numerous darts trophies. But the early morning dew on his boots, the fowls scratching on the back doorstep, the evocative smell of wet cows in the byre reached out to him like some unseen umbilical, drawing him home. It had been so with his Father and his Father before him, so it should come as no great surprise that the working knowledge of sophisticated forms of birth control were well outside his compass. To a man, whose very apex of *savoir faire* was the illicit snaring of a couple of rabbits, anything more technical than the simple withdrawal method was stone cold anathema. Although, in fairness to him, he had heard sketchy details down at his 'local' some years previously of something known as the rhythm method. He had, uncharacteristically, flirted with it briefly, until, in the first grey light of some winter's dawn, mistaking its shadowy form for that of his jangling alarm clock, he had brought a great ham fist roundly down upon the metronome sitting on his bedside table. It disintergrated. From that moment on Father was a withdrawal man through and through.

It was this fact, on a wartime evening when Wellingtons were Junkers and Bristolians slept blissfully in their beds, that was to be

Father's abject undoing. For, at that very moment, when eyes cross, colours fuse, neons flash and myriad tinsel-winged fritillaries dance before cascading torrents of incandescence, he instinctively lurched backwards, striking his left buttock squarely on the corner of the electricity meter. Uttering a profane oath, he recoiled in pained surprise, and Mother was with child.

I was not present to verify the happenings of that fateful evening, but can thank the siting of the electricity meter for my very existence.

Father was apparently less than ecstatic when learning of the result of his sexual *faux-pas*. At first he took a considerable amount of convincing. His initial reaction was to accuse the local G.P. of cost cutting by laying in a duff batch of litmus paper, and following this by laying the blame for Mother's morning sickness squarely at the door of wartime rationed dried egg. Even more surprised was Mother herself. As she recounted to a neighbour later, she had long considered herself, now aged thirty-nine, as incapable of having children. Upon reflection, she thought she probably owed her shock conception to a pig. Her neighbour hastily bid her not to be too uncharitable, as at times Father could be passably civil. Unheeding, Mother bore on, recounting an episode that occured some three weeks prior to the by now discredited 'air-raid'. Helping, as she did, to tend the numerous pigs at Father's place of employ, she had on the afternoon at issue, armed only with a bucketful of swill, clambered into the pen of a sow with her litter. Taking exception to the intruding figure, even if it was carrying lunch, the old sow trundled forward with rancorous intent, spreadeagling all seven stones of Mother into the mire. Despite its repeated attempts to root and gore her, she had managed eventually to extricate herself from the foul smelling morass and regain the safety of the fence.

"I felt something go, I know I did!" she assured her sceptical neighbour. Down there, y'know where them sort of things do go! Frank don't believe me," she continued, "but I'm worried, I think that pig's an ill omen. It's going to affect the baby I know it is!" Despite the neighbour's half-hearted effort to reassure her she carried on in train, "Like them women what see hares run across in front of 'em when 'ems expectin' and the baby's born with a hare lip. 'E's goin' to 'ave summat of the pig about 'un I just know he is!"

Now whether she envisaged me being born with a little pink snout, a curly tail, an apple in my mouth or clutching six pen'orth of brawn wrapped in greaseproof paper, I've never managed to ascertain. But, as to date, I have never been approached by a single wholesale pork butcher, I think we can safely assume that she was mistaken. The decision that has faced all prospective parents, that of naming the little wombful when it emerged, was made relatively easy for them by an act of kindness they'd performed some years previously. They had occasion to look after a cairn terrier for a friend. So taken with the little chap were they, that they'd vowed if ever they had a son he should be named after it. The dog's name was Toby, and all my life I've borne a certain deep seated gratitude that they never had cause to stable a seventeen hands Clydesdale gelding called Dobbin!

The Fiveways Maternity Hospital in Yeovil was the venue for my arrival onto the stage of life. Father was not present, excusing himself with,

"Ah! Done too many bloody calvin's t'bide an' mess about wi' that!".

However, in fairness to him, he did ring up to enquire, and after work cycled the three miles into town just to see what the vagaries of nature had brought him.

Apparently he arrived in the ward still wearing his cycle clips, sporting a couple of bits of fag paper camouflaging two shaving nicks just above his 'Adams apple', and with a reed-thin 'home roll', which, although extinguished by the cycle ride, still adhered doggedly to his bottom lip.

Mother watched in disbelief as, obviously well pleased with his urbane appearance, he sidled across the ward to where a blonde lady of ample endowment was cradling an infant in her arms. The colour rose in her cheeks as Father positioned himself, ostensibly to admire the child, but in so doing, affording himself altogether wider and more stimulating vistas. He engaged her all the while with trivial banalities, whilst from his bottom lip the scrawny little dog-end dangled racily.

He felt a firm grip just above his elbow, and turned to find himself gazing into the florid face and cool grey eyes of the Ward Sister.

"Your wife and child are over here Mr Dyer! " she said pointedly. Maintaining her grip she propelled Father gently but firmly towards the bed occupied by Mother.

Being met with a scowl, he rallied lamely with "Thought she were the wife of a chap I d'play darts wi' down the Masons Arms!

"Well" he said taking on a conciliatory tone "lets 'ave a look at the little bugger then!" Mother leaned over and withdrew some of the swaddling.

Father gazed down at the tiny face, wrinkled like a rubescent walnut, and suddenly a strange far-away look stole into his eyes. He realized, that for as long as he could remember, he'd always wanted a really good cow-dog.

My formative years were spent playing musical cottages all over the South West of England. Father was an agricultural labourer, a cow-man to be more precise, with a very short fuse. Not only would he brook no nonsense, as often as not he would brook no reason. He also observed a dubious philosophy where work was concerned, of 'always leaving a bit for tomorrow'. The combination of these two factors, allied as they were to a 'tied cottage' situation, ensured that during those years we rarely stayed anywhere long enough for the mail from our previous address to catch up with us.

I had an uncle from Chichester, a driver for Pickfords, who, when he could find us, sometimes dropped in on one of his return journeys. So I knew from an early age what a furniture van looked like. It was large, capacious, dry inside, and smelt faintly of camphor.

I couldn't help feeling that with all our moves, we must be prime candidates for a furniture van. But no. What arrived each time to collect our humble sticks was large, capacious, wet inside, and smelt strongly of cow dung. To be fair the various drivers, having completed their Friday market runs had sluiced a few buckets of water around to make things more acceptable, but there was no camouflaging the smell of the cow house, or the caked manure that, more often than not, clung tenaciously to the ventilation slots in the vehicle's sides.

To Father, removal days were little more than an irksome inconvenience, to Mother they were pure trauma. Mattresses rolled, bedding in bundles, pictures stacked, a hessian sack between each and tied with twine. Crockery, glass and ornaments wrapped in newspapers were carefully placed in numerous oval zinc baths of varying sizes.

Mother would scurry around twittering and wringing her hands as her precious chattels were hoicked up into the lorry with great gusto. Despite all her care in packing, the family china became progressively more chipped and dog-eared with each move. Ornaments in particular seemed to bear the brunt. Three-legged animals of various species seemed the norm, and the spectre of the headless milkmaid fondly embracing a one-eared airedale is with me still.

To this day I'm still not totally convinced that the Venus di Milo wasn't, at some stage, subjected to at least a couple of moves with my parents.

The furniture was best described as sturdy and utilitarian, good old four square tables and chairs built to withstand repeated trips up and down cattle lorry tail ramps. Splintering noises were still fairly commonplace, but a smartly hammered two-inch nail was always a sovereign remedy. Father was very buccaneer about the whole thing. The only piece of furniture that commanded respect was the china cabinet, and about this he was totally paranoid.

He was convinced that the lead light windowing at its front and sides was of a construction —

"What can't be done no more! Cos the skill 'ave died out and they've took their secret wi'um!" What he conveniently saw fit to overlook when imbuing this masterpiece with heady mystique, was that he'd purchased it new in a department store in Portsmouth in 1928. But the myth was perpetuated and the precious piece swaddled in numerous hessian sacks was carried and placed with great reverence onto the dank and malodorous lorry bed. Unfortunately, cattle lorries lurching along undulating, pot-hole strewn, country roads bear scant respect for extinct glazing skills. So, pane by pane, one move at a time, and to Father's gathering chagrin the 'priceless' workmanship disintegrated. Both sides came eventually to be clad in green curtain material, and although later reglazed, it was only in plain glass.

Still the cabinet puffed out its chest, as, stuffed with odd pieces of Goss china, plastic gewgaws, darts trophies and sundry ornamental paraphernalia, it commanded the deference due to its exalted position of family heirloom supreme. Father was always at pains to impress upon me that if I did not go through life 'keeping my nose clean' come the Judgement Day this precious piece just might not be coming my way. And so it hung over my head, like the very sword of Damocles.

All the hoary old chestnuts about 'cold air rushing out to meet you as the front door is opened in a blizzard' and 'condensation forming on the outside of windows' were probably penned by someone who had lived in at least one of the cottages we occupied.

They invariably bore the same hallmarks — cracked walls, sagging ceilings, rising damp, descending damp, and no cooking facilities other than Mother's venerable paraffin stove. A perfunctory water supply, usually consisting of a single cold tap with a banging air lock that dripped constantly onto a brown stain in the chipped enamel sink. Certainly no bathroom, perish the very thought, and the outside privy, at the far end of the garden cowering neath a festoon of brambles. True, when we first set foot inside, these humble dwellings were cold, miserable, damp and depressing. But once we'd unpacked our homely effects and settled in as a family unit, somehow it all seemed so very much worse.

Mother, armed with only her trusty Valor paraffin stove, would take the lowliest cuts of meat, simple, fresh vegetables from the garden, and, with culinary skills garnered over the years, conjure up something the dog wouldn't look at.

Her one concession to the moderately discerning human palate was her bacon and onion roly-poly. Tasty and sustaining, it formed just one tiny atoll in a vast ocean of gastronomic mediocrity. Even in those early years I could always sense when another move was imminent. Father would be seen restlessly scanning the 'situations vacant' column of the *Western Gazette*. Some days later I would be hurriedly dragged into the kitchen by Mother as yet another ruddy-faced gentleman in brown twill trousers and loud tweed jacket faced Father across the living room table.

Sure enough, within days the china was back in the zinc baths and the pictures back in their hessian sacks. The milkmaid, her head now clumsily glued back on, and her lily-white neck displaying a dark brown ring of surplus glue, looked for all the world as though she'd been brutally garrotted with a silk scarf liberally coated in Marmite. Because her head had slipped from position whilst the glue was setting she now gazed askance at her trusty airedale companion, who, with a look of glum resignation, remained, sadly earless. Both were enveloped in numerous pages of the *Daily Mirror*, and carefully placed next to the china 'dancing pig', who had lost the offside fore leg and his piccolo in a calamitous coming together with the one quart teapot a couple of moves previously.

And so the scene was oft times repeated. Each time Father reassured us that this would be the job into which he would settle.

"Beautiful little cottage too!" he would say, "All mod cons, couldn't wish fer better! Got a decent bloke t' move us these time an' all, none o' yer bloody fly-by-night 'auliers!"

With scarcely a moment to digest the glad tidings, the light was suddenly blotted from the kitchen window. The cattle lorry had arrived.

I suppose I had reached an age when various outside influences were beginning to colour the light in which I was viewing both my parents and our eccentric, semi-nomadic way of life. I was realizing that most of my peers had lived all of six or so years in their present surroundings. They often resented an interloper suddenly crawling from the depths of a cattle lorry into their midst. Being accepted called for one long round of ingratiation and appeasement, which no sooner achieved was called for again at our next transitory port of call.

In my Father, I was beginning to identify a talent for embarrassing and discomposing that was all the time being brought more sharply into relief. As an individual he was brash and awkward, whilst at the same time vain and ingenious. His past-mastery at conjuring up acutely embarrassing situations could not be questioned, and a whole litany of these were to bedevil my early life.

The earliest I clearly recall was at the age of about six and a half, when living in the small Somerset hamlet of Lullington, near Frome. Father had just seen fit to threaten his boss with an 'arse first trip into the dung pile!' This of course spelt further hazard for the china milkmaid and her merry, mutilated band. This time however, we weren't to throw our humble possessions into a cattle lorry, as there wasn't one available. What there was available was a flat-bed lorry.

The move was to be ten or so miles to Woolley Grange near Bradford-on-Avon. Fortunately the weather was bright and sunny, which was more that could be said for Mother's disposition. Mattresses and bedding stained by dung water were one thing, but the prospect of having a high percentage of her worldly goods scattered haphazardly along the length of the B3109 was another, and it filled her with a mounting anxiety. Berating Father was as so much water off a ducks back.

"Bugger it woman!" he replied, "we've got enough rope 'ere to rig a bloody three-master!"

She was less than convinced. Nor were her anxieties diminished by the groups of neighbours leaning on gates and walls sagely observing the domestic melodrama unfolding before them. In quiet rural backwaters, before Desmond Lynham made them his own, Saturday afternoons offered little in the way of entertainment, so this was high theatre indeed. Each item, as it was carried from house to truck, received caustic appraisal. Had they held aloft score cards for technical merit and artistic interpretation it would hardly have surprised. Sniggerings and chortlings rose intermittently to guffaws of ribald laughter, as lances of bucolic wit struck home.

Like a nervous peewit, her floral pinny flapping in the breeze, Mother flitted around smiling appeasingly at her audience. Father enquired in elemental Anglo-Saxon whether, perhaps, there was some other business they could be attending to. But they had their seats in the front row of the stalls and no amount of appeasement or vitriol was going to dislodge them.

Eventually, roped from every conceivable angle, and reminiscent of a scene from *The Grapes of Wrath*, everything was on board and we were ready for off. Mother was in the cab next to the driver with me balanced on her knee. Father was on the back wedged into one of the threadbare armchairs, clutching onto a short length of binder twine, the other end of which was threaded through the collar of Bruce, the border collie, the nearest that Father was ever to get to his utopian dream of a 'really good cow-dog'. The rest of the menagerie – two cats and a crateful of squawking hens – kept him company.

To the sounds of ironic clapping, and someone ringing a bicycle bell in frenzied salute, we trundled off up the road. Contrary to Mother's forebodings not a single stick, pot or utensil escaped from Father's 'cat's cradle' of ropes. All went uncharacteristically well until we reached the town centre of Bradford-on-Avon itself.

It was mid-afternoon and there appeared to be a disquieting absence of vehicles. True, there were a lot of people about, more perhaps than one might usually expect for a Saturday afternoon's shopping. But for all that, it appeared that the shopkeepers might not grow too fat from their numbers, as they weren't busily milling about and darting into shops. They were standing still in ranks, three or four deep in places, on the pavement on both sides of the street. What had not been realised until that moment was that we'd chosen to move on Bradford-on-Avon's carnival day, and we were just about the last vehicle through before the road was closed for the procession. There may have been no entry number on the vehicle but that wasn't about to stop an expectant crowd enjoying it.

To people who had always known the good fortune of having their furnishings transported in something large, capacious and dry inside that smelt faintly of camphor, we must have presented a jolly spectacle indeed. Ribald comments issued forth from one or two of the inebriates in the crowd.

"Cor! Polish refugees eh? Very good, very authentic!"

"What 'appened to the rest of the waggon train, been ambushed by Comanches?" and other barbed shafts in similar vein, soon extracted sardonic laughter, whistles, and mocking applause from the packed pavements. I peered through the back window to see Father with a weak smile, attempting to parry some of the taunts. His lame attempts at witty riposte were suddenly cut short by Bruce lunging, hackles raised, fangs bared, in the direction of someone to whom he had taken exception. Father, catapulted from his armchair, fought desperately to restrain the dog, whilst maintaining some vestige of composure and dignity on the lurching lorry bed.

Bruce lunged, hackles raised, fangs bared.

His troubles were, however, only beginning, as the sudden violent movements, allied to the cacophony from the roadside spooked the crateful of chickens, whose state of panic added strident squawks, dust and feathers to the furore. Simultaneously, two hitherto dormant hessian sacks began jerking and bouncing around the floor. Father, in time-honoured tradition, always transported his cats in tied hessian sacks and these two had now been thrown into a

17

paroxysm of fear.

With the dog now lapsing into foaming dementia he had cast all pretence of composure to the four winds, as, with face contorted and suffused with rage he uttered unseemly oaths whilst performing an animated hornpipe around the lorry bed in a vain attempt to place his foot on the necks of the cartwheeling sacks. By this time sections of the crowd were hooting their approval. A few even succumbed to the old carnival tradition of casting nobbins onto the truck. The coins clattering around him did nothing to humour Father, or to temper his profanities. It had degenerated into pure farce.

I recall it was at that moment, for the first time in my young life, that I experienced the feeling of true gut-curdling embarrassment. I desperately wanted the lorry footwell to open up and swallow me, in the way I was going to wish a variety of surfaces to assimilate me over the years to come. The churlish, weathered face of the lorry driver cracked into a gap-toothed grin.

"Shall I slow down a bit more?" he chuckled, "Frank's doing quite well with the small change back there," he then added pointedly, "If 'er kips goin' at these rate I might get a tip out of 'im these time." Mother sat tight-lipped and responded not a bit.

Slowly we eased our way up the hill and out of the town, Bruce calmed down, the two hessian sacks subsided, and you could almost hear the groans of the onlookers, sensing that the true gem of the parade had passed, and was gone.

Much imagination and effort had been put into the floats that were to follow but they'd be hard pressed to match the warm-up act.

2.
Daffodils, Roll-ups and
the Queensberry Rules

THRIFT AND CHASTISEMENT were the edicts of the household. Ours was a very low-key economy: not much coming in – virtually nothing going out. Mother saw to it that the kitchen ran on a monastic frugality that ensured nothing was wasted and very little savoured. The Sunday joint was often stretched to cover six days. Fatty pieces of brisket lurked hot, beneath the leaden Yorkshire, on the Sabbath. Cold and unappetising, it sidled up to bubble and squeak on Monday. On Tuesday minced remnants, mixed with left-over bubble and squeak, onion and swede, cowered under a stodgy thatch of mashed potato, producing an equally unappetising prospect, optimistically called cottage pie. Wednesday saw remaining oddments stewed up with corned beef and onion into a sort of horrendous hash and eaten with bread and dripping. On Thursday the bone and gristle took centre stage, having been simmered for anything up to twenty-four hours to produce a dismal workhouse broth. Basically a bowl of discoloured water on which floated an eddying slick of grease, which, if leaked into the Bristol Channel, would have spelled a miserable end for countless sea birds. To this unpromising basic Mother added mini dumplings, peas and carrots. After a day when fresh air and exercise had honed the appetite to a keen edge this rather daunting concoction proved surprisingly unpalatable.

The role of the joint on its sixth day was always shrouded in mystery. I was firmly convinced, however, that its final remains were minced with liberal dollops of bloater paste and served up as those revolting soggy fishcakes that regularly put in a Friday appearance.

Perfectly edible cabbage was left bubbling on the stove for an age, until the house reeked of it, resulting in a flavourless sludge in the bottom of the saucepan. All this to produce, if my Mother is to be believed, better cabbage water with which to mix the glutinous

19

substance passed off as gravy, that clung mulishly to every surface it touched.

Cheese was another foodstuff which baffled me in my early years. It wasn't the wide variety of types and flavours that confused me for at that time I had only ever come face to face with the ubiquitous Cheddar. But so often, with my nose propped just above the counter, I'd watch owl-eyed as old Mrs Brister at the village shop eased the taut wire through the mellow, mouthwatering slab. Pausing only to readjust her spectacles as they slid down her nose, she removed a slice and placed it, along with her thumb, onto the scales. This substance was moist and crumbly, it smelt nutty and piquant. I watched intently. No, there was no sleight of hand, the slice of cheese was definitely enveloped in greaseproof paper, and the greaseproof package slid into the paper bag. Yes, Mother did take it from the counter and place it atop the tin of marrowfat peas in her string bag. So it was going home with us.

Back in our kitchen that very same paper bag left the string bag and was placed in the wooden and perforated zinc meat 'safe'. So, how come, when it was hauled out for supper, this moist, crumbly, nutty delicacy had transformed itself into a dry and cracked brick, with an oily texture to its outer skin and a dank and musty taste.

The answer was to be found, I eventually discovered, in thrift and self perpetuation. Mother's thrift-riddled brain would only countenance the buying, each Saturday, of exactly enough cheese to last the following week. It also dictated that under no circumstances should the new cheese be started before old stocks were exhausted. But somewhere back along the misty paths of time she'd been forced, by some cataclysmic event or other to abandon her consumption routine by starting a piece of cheese in midweek. Blinkered by self imposed custom she could not abandon her buying routine, thus the whole thing was thrown totally out of sync.

The cheese languished for four days exposed to the air, dispelling all of its moisture and delicacy of flavour long before it put in an appearance at the supper table. Consequently, as this situation appeared self perpetuating, our tastebuds weekly enacted a penance to the principles of habitual parsimony.

Another basic staple that bedevilled me at this time was bread. A simple enough commodity you might think, but not when you're seven and your Uncle Wilf manages a butcher's shop in Frome. You see, compared to us, Uncle Wilf was rolling in it. He lived behind the shop and enjoyed all the perks. Never any need for his family to stretch a piece of fatty brisket over six days. Free use of the firm's van was taken for granted and they actually had a television set, with an enormous magnifying glass strapped to the front. This always ensured everyone watched in a huddle directly in front of the screen. Watching from a slight angle you risked bizarre picture distortion. I've seen the Range Rider's hat stretch to three times the length of his horse.

But, I hear you ask, what has the Range Rider's headware got to do with my perplexities concerning bread? Well, not a lot, truth be told, save that he was normally dashing about with his partner tidying up the Old West when we arrived by bus for tea, as we occassionally did. There was always a feeling that Uncle Wilf, pricked by some underlying family conscience, looked upon these visits as an act of benign charity. Certainly the sitting room table always groaned under a formidable array of cakes, biscuits, trifle, salad, cold meats and pies that would help to fuel us through a few more sparse weeks. As often as not I was called in from the kitchen, where I had been sitting wistfully coveting the contents of the bowl their dog had disdainfully pushed aside.

Breasting the table I was afforded vistas of gastronomic enrapturement. I needed little bidding to be in amongst it, arms a blur, piling my plate, until eventually replete I sank back quietly, the stomach sending up fretful messages of disquiet. But for all the comparative richness of the fare, it wasn't the meat pies, the cakes, nor even the cream laden trifle that delighted my youthful palate; it was the bread and butter, cut neatly into triangles from corner to corner. It was delicious! Why had my own Mother not stumbled across this secret? Why did she persist in cutting slices of bread and butter straight across leaving two rectangular pieces, when cut from corner to corner in two triangles it tasted so demonstrably better? Slice after slice of bread I buttered, cutting each piece with measured precision from corner to corner. But no matter how carefully cut, the result was always the same, the taste was flat and lifeless.

Why, I puzzled, should bread cut triangularly taste differently from that cut rectangularly and why only at Uncle Wilf's? I remained baffled. It was some years before the answer finally dawned on me. At Uncle Wilf's they had spread butter. Mother always bought margarine.

Father was also sucked into this grey vacuum of thrift. The

occasional packet of Woodbines would pass through his hands, but he was an arch devotee of the 'home-roll'. A much dented baccy tin, polished to a lustre by years of residence in his jacket pocket, contained his requisite supply of Golden Virginia and a packet of Rizla Red fag papers. These were habitually hauled out at dinner times. Whilst awaiting his tilt at Mother's gastronomic assault course, he would steady himself by indulging in his main roll-up of the day.

Framed in the kitchen doorway on a steel cold January day, he'd truculently kick off his wellington boots before shuffling the few paces and sinking into a kitchen chair. With elbows planted firmly on the table top supporting hunched shoulders, he absently blew warm air into frost-numbed hands cupped before him. Minutes later he'd stir, a corpulent dew drop still hanging crystalline and pendant from his hawk-like nose, and produce the revered baccy tin from the depths of his pocket.

Two factors governed Father's rolling activities. Firstly his determination to keep baccy consumption down to a minimum, and secondly his hands. Nature, God bless her, had issued him with very large, square hands, and years of manual labour had further accentuated their musculature, along with robbing them of sensitivity and dexterity. Calloused and chapped, they were wielded like two great meaty shovels. The thick, heavy fingers were very reminiscent of a clump of dahlia tubers. Armed with these unpromisingly cumbersome tools, the art of rolling his own should have been beyond him. But surprisingly not so.

As he fumbled awkwardly to extract a paper and a fid of baccy he would drift quietly onto automatic pilot. His face took on a glassy-eyed, reptilian expression. His tongue flicked out spasmodically like that of an inquisitive slow-worm, moistening the rolled paper, as his mind drifted contemplatively to the following Thursday's darts match. Elbows on table, two enormous hands opposed at chin level clumsily fumbling his task, he often looked for all the world like a huge, bellicose shore-crab struggling in vain to come to terms with the finer intricacies of petit point. The whole routine was enacted in silence, as Mother was usually engrossed in sieving lumps out of the gravy. Any stray strands at the ends were plucked out, dropping to the table top or floor and accumulating with the rest that had been spilt during rolling. Consequently, there was usually more baccy around Father's feet than in the roll-ups. The finished products were lamentable, scrawny things, more paper than tobacco. When lit they burned at an alarming rate, and came to be known over the years as Father's 7-second fuses.

The dog-ends left after such burn-ups, although pitifully small, were 'endearingly' placed behind the ear to be kept for later. Long years of habit enabled him to wedge two or three behind each ear, until such time as they could be broken down and the few remaining strands of baccy recovered and recycled.

Any tendency on my part to be feckless and spendthrift was also stamped on very heavily, as was graphically illustrated on Mother's Day 1952. I was moved, for some unfathomable reason, to do what little boys are supposed to do for Mums on such a day. I contrived to make a card using pencil and crayons. I had also mustered together one shilling and sixpence from donations by Gran and an abnormally charitable Aunt. This sum I'd earmarked for some flowers.

Early that Sunday morning I melted quietly from the house, making my way through the churchyard to a small-holding which lay on the main road at its far side. There was a board I'd noticed a few days previously, propped at an angle against the stone wall. 'DAFFS FOR SALE' it proclaimed. Clutching my money in hot little palm I knocked nervously at a side door, alongside which stood half a dozen buckets crammed with daffodils and narcissi. The door was opened by old Mr Ashworth, whom I knew by sight.

"Ah – Dyer's young lad from the bailiffs cottage ain't you, and what be you after?"

"Flowers for Mother's day!" I replied, shifting awkwardly, and colouring at the sound of my own voice.

"How many dus want?"

"I've only got one and six." I told him.

"Right, I'll mix you up some of these bigguns and some narcissus." he said, taking handfuls from various buckets. He hastily tied a length of twine around them, snipped the end off with his clasp knife, and held them up at arms length admiringly. "Aint that just a handsome bunch?" he smiled "I hope she likes 'em my boy." I handed over my money and, with scarce a 'Thank you', I scampered back across the road, and fairly tore through the churchyard, hoping against hope that none of the kids from the village would see me.

I was in luck. I reached the house and sneaked around the side into the toolshed. Hiding the flowers under a sack, I crept indoors and up to my bedroom where I collected the card and a length of coloured raffia I'd hoarded. Back in the shed I removed the length of plain twine, rearranged the blooms into what I considered a more attractive bunch and carefully bound them again with the coloured raffia. I slipped the card inside the raffia, braced myself, and marched purposefully into the kitchen. Mother, her back to me, was at the sink, energetically scraping one of her gourmet creations out of a large saucepan.

'Where the hell did you pinch them from?'

She turned as I piped up, 'Happy Mother's day Mum!' Wiping her hands perfunctorily on her pinny, she started to say,

"But those are really lovely." She never, as I recall, quite finished the statement before it was drowned out by a bellow from behind me.

"Where the hell did you pinch them from?" Father's towering frame filled the doorway.

"I never did, I bought them," I replied, fortified with a slight inner confidence, born of the knowledge that at least I was within the law of the land.

"Bought 'em, what with?" he queried.

"Some money I got from Gran!" My confidence was waning. "Oh yea, and where can you buy flowers around here on a Sunday?" He was glowering now, not a good sign.

"Mr Ashworth's, over on the main road." I felt the noose was tightening.

"And how much did 'e charge thee for they?"

"One and six," I replied, hopefully.

"One and bloody six!" he roared. "Right, let's have them flowers 'ere. You come wi me my boy!" So saying, he whipped the flowers from Mother's grasp. She recoiled, but managed to clutch on to the card.

Father gripped me roughly by the upper arm as we stormed out of the house. All the way through the churchyard Father muttered darkly. I couldn't help feeling that for some reason Mr Ashworth was going to wish he was away visiting relatives this Sunday.

Father's ham fist beat a staccato roll on Mr Ashworths door. Just before the hinges capitulated, the door opened halfway and Mr Ashworth's benevolent face appeared.

"Yes?" he said meekly.

"One and bloody six," Father bawled, "That's what you stung my boy for these 'ere daffodils!" Mr Ashworth opened his mouth to respond, but was given no chance. "You got a bloody great orchard diggered wi um 'ere!" No one could deny Father's observations were correct. Beneath bare-limbed fruit trees hundreds, if not thousands of daffodils and narcissi nodded to each other in neighbourly cordiality.

"You must think we're made o' money or bloody daft!" By now he was in awesome tirade.

"Well I um, its um, well," countered Mr Ashworth feebly.

"Well nothing!" intoned Father grabbing the opportunity to introduce a little continuity. "Well here's your soddin flowers," he said, ramming them back in a bucket, still bound in my precious length of coloured raffia.

"I'll 'ave my boy's one and a tanner back now!"

Mr Ashworth fumbled deep in his trouser pocket, eventually coming up with three sixpenny pieces. On handing them over he said appeasingly,

"I am sorry you feel upset!"

"Not now we'me got our bloody money back I don't!" replied Father, and we left.

Walking back again through the churchyard Father lectured me sternly. "Next time you do get the urge to bide an' drow money about on thik kind o' rubbish, thee's ask I first. There's plenty of sly buggers about that'll 'ave thee pocket linings fer snot rags, soon as look at thee; use yer noddle and save a bit. There's heaps o' primroses along under Pickets Copse 'edge, get up there an' pick a few o' they!" I considered asking for my one and six back, thought better of it, and reassured myself that there would be a more opportune moment.

We arrived back at the house to find Mother in the living room. "I do hope you weren't rude to him, Frank," she said, placing my crayoned card carefully on the mantlepiece.

A salutary lesson had been learned; indeed, it was about this time that Father seemed to take an uncustomarily keen interest in my education. Not, I hasten to add, that of a scholastic nature, but an education best described as having a 'worldly' slant. Such priceless pieces of tuition as the correct way to daub mud and moss on freshly cut tree stumps in the wood to camouflage the illicit felling of firewood. The salient points of constructing a pheasant fence in the copse, an operation carried out furtively on a Sunday morning. It entailed the erecting of a fence some three feet high of interlocking brushwood, running the width of the copse. At intervals, gaps were left and in each of these was placed a wire snare attached to a whippy sapling, bent and pegged.

At dusk we'd return, steadily moving through the copse rattling a box of matches. Great emphasis was placed on not moving too urgently and panicking the pheasants into flight. Scurrying on before us, the hapless birds soon found the gaps in the fence. Snares triggered, they were shot up into the air, where they were quickly gathered by Father who, chortling with delight, stuffed them into a hessian sack.

Expert coaching was also on hand for such nefarious pastimes as noosing roosting pheasants with longpole and horse hair loop. Long-netting rabbits, which saw us employing a moonlit night with scudding black clouds to stealthily peg out twenty yards of net between foraging rabbits and their warren, before Father leapt into the air like a scalded wallaby, scaring them headlong into it. We took a look at ferretting, and probing the stream bed for eels with a four-grained prong, and perhaps most quaintly at 'floating' a moorhen's nest. Father held a very high regard for the eggs of both peewits and moorhens as a breakfast delicacy, and in securing the eggs of the latter exhibited a patience and forbearance quite foreign to his character.

Cutting a forked hazel sapling he would ease it out across the water to where the moorhen had nested on a partially submerged branch. Slowly he inched the fork beneath the nest. Then, ever so gingerly, wrested it from its moorings. It was then the work of moments to float it, complete with its cargo of dappled eggs, back to the bank. Moorhen's eggs were far too rich for my young palate. But with their yolk oozing in sluggish, deep golden rivulets down the stubbly contours of his chin, they represented, for Father, an unparalleled breakfast treat.

Strangely enough, it was the chin that was to be the very kernel of my next piece of home tutelage.

"Protect it at all times," instructed Father, as he landed a long left lead plumb on my forehead. He had decreed that for the purposes of 'self defence' I should be grounded in the basic rudiments of the noble art, and who better to instruct me. Father had an almost encyclopaedic knowledge of boxing. He would constantly drop the names of Jack Dempsey, Gene Tunney and Jimmy Wilde into the conversation as though they were chaps with whom he'd been enjoying a convivial pint at the White Lion the previous weekend.

He would never miss a big fight broadcast, decreeing total silence from Mother and myself for its duration. This presented no great hardship for me, as I was always royally entertained by his antics. Mother, who had over the years become totally blasé about the whole thing, sat in a state of blissful detachment, on the opposite side of the fireplace, quietly crocheting yet another cerise cat flap curtain.

Father leant forward expectantly in his armchair. Knuckles blanched, fingers nervously digging into the arm rests, his ear strained towards the venerable faltering wireless set as he soaked up the tension of the big fight preliminaries. The bell sounded, and he was galvanised into action. With his backside still rooted firmly in the chair, he bobbed and weaved, pawed the air with a succession of left leads, then smartly ducking an imaginary right hook delivered his own chopping right counter. All the while his lips were animatedly mouthing the commentator's words. It was an unfortunate trait of Fathers. He was one of those whose lips moved whilst other people were reading.

By this time the radio valves were glowing white hot, and the fight moving on apace. Father held both fists to his temples in a clever defensive manoeuvre and was just about to unleash a telling right to the solar plexus when the bell sounded for the end of the round. He slumped back in his chair, small beads of perspiration clearly evident on his forehead and his breathing deep and laboured.

"Bloody fool!" he panted, "Buggered if I know what he thinks he's doing! Up on his soddin' toes dancin' around like some bloody nancy boy!"

"Tea dear?" queried Mother.

"Got no idea," continued Father, "Never ought to be in for a title. Got knocked arse over 'ead last time 'e fought a Yank!"

"Bit o' bread an' drippin' or a cake?" solicited Mother.

"Stood up there pawing out a left. No good hittin' these blackies in the 'ead. Downstairs, that's where 'e wants to go, they don't like it in the breadbasket!"

"Right, so that's tea and a bit o' bread an' drippin'!" concluded Mother, and shuffled off to the kitchen as the bell sounded for the second.

It was during one of Father's earlier armchair contests that Thomas, our streetwise but affable feline eunuch, came rather unstuck. He was sitting on the arm of the chair next to Father, feet tucked beneath his chest, eyes closed, a blissful smile wreathing his countenance. Bathed, as he was, in the warm glow from the fire his whiskers twitched as he succumbed to drifting reverie – sun-dappled pastures, alive with field mice; slow, easily caught field mice; tempting sparrows with wings in splints. A fat, succulent rat on an iron lung. He was awash with chimera. The bell sounding for round one of the long-awaited European bantamweight clash elicited no more than a part rotation of one crenellated ear in the general direction of the wireless. He was oblivious to the fact that even now Father was fighting a particularly action-packed opening round.

Forced to clinch twice on the ropes, he was under considerable pressure; nevertheless, lightning reflexes enabled him to slip a tentative left lead, feint with his own left, and knock his opponent temporarily off balance with a crisp right. Sensing the opening, Father unleashed a tigerish haymaker. Thomas was airborne for scarce a second, as, jolted from his reverie by the force of the blow, he spun headlong into the fireplace. Still bemused, he sat amongst the fire irons blinking uncomprehendingly. Suddenly, he remembered just what mean and predatory cats were meant to do when called upon to show their mettle. The bloodcurdling wail of a banshee rent the air, and a black and white blur traversed the flagstone floor, disappearing beneath the couch. From that day Thomas could be seen taking his ease in the comparative safety of the dirty linen basket. A contented smile creasing his chops, whiskers gently twitching, but one green eye remaining warily ajar, ever watchful for the pay-off punch.

Father's boxing experience came from his naval days. He had once been detailed onto a fatigue party erecting the ring for an inter-dockyard match. However, he wasn't about to let this detract from the enthusiasm he was to exhibit in coaching his only son.

In stockinged feet, he danced around the kitchen floor, shoulders hunched and with a look of venomous intent on his face. "C'mon!" he taunted. "Try an' 'it me!" I was still three feet out of range when a great clenched fist caught me on the bridge of the nose. Incensed, I stormed forwards.

"Don't forget yer defence!" were the last words I remember hearing, as a clubbing right caught me somewhere on the temple. The curtains and the fireplace suddenly changed places, and I recall the hideous unglazed print entitled 'Highland cattle at Loch Loyne' multiplying ten fold and chasing each other at speed around the walls. I came to, with Mother kneeling over me clutching a bloodstained towel.

"Are you alright?" she quizzed, a rare look of concern furrowing her brow.

"Course 'es alright!" advised Father. "I only gave 'im a tap!"

I had to admit I didn't feel too 'alright'. I could feel blood trickling slowly down my throat, and the impression of a large, cold door key between my shoulder blades.

"It's only a soddin' nosebleed!" said Father dismissively. "Wait till it eases up an' I'll show 'im 'ow to block a right 'ook!"

Father was obviously keen to continue the class. He was up on his toes shadow-boxing menacingly. Snorting and flicking the side of his nose with his thumb, he feinted to his left and threw a quick combination at an imaginary opponent. Mother rounded on him like an infuriated Jack Russell. "You're so bloody clumsy!" she shrieked "You get carried away. Y'don't know your own strength!"

Laying there I was forced to agree. At six-foot-one and thirteen-

and-a-half stone he was a formidable opponent for a seven-year-old.

"We're having no more of this nonsense and that's an end to it," chided Mother, her hackles still vertically inclined.

"Dear oh dear" droned Father sardonically. "First sight of a drop o' claret an' 'is corner pulls 'im out! Right nancy boy 'ell turn out if 'e carries on like that!"

Boxing tuition was never resumed, and I think it came as a great disappointment to Father that a pair of gloves were not on my wanted list for the following Christmas. I opted instead for a bird book and a football. Mind you, I had opted for a football the previous Christmas and received a torch and plastic hen that laid eggs when its body was depressed.

Mother had this disconcerting tendency of throwing herself into Christmas a bit. Nothing too over the top. A few 'lick-your-own' coloured paper chains, a wire framed ivy ball hanging in a corner decorated with three strands of tinsel and a tired fairy, with a yellowing tutu and a bent wand, were about all she could muster. Although to be fair she did annually boil up a couple of Christmas puddings, through which we eagerly searched for concealed silver threepenny pieces, before abandoning the rest on the side of the plate.

Father, on the other hand, held no brief at all for Christmas, and was very surly about the 'season of good will'. Anyone standing on our front door-step offering a slightly off-key rendition of 'Little Town of Bethlehem' got very short shrift indeed. Nor did he relish the link between presents and his purse.

Going outside the back door on Christmas Eve, discharging both barrels of his shotgun, then coming back in to announce, "Sorry son, it's goin' to be a lean Christmas. Santa's just shot himself!" never really occurred to him. But my God, how he wished it had.

One earlier Christmas Eve Mother had given me one of Father's voluminous 'wellington' socks to hang on the bed end. Too excited to sleep, I was suddenly aware of a shaft of light cutting in from the landing. Feigning sleep but with one eye squinting over the army surplus blanket, I watched with mounting anticipation as a shadowy form slunk into the room. It creaked across the bare boards with all the stealth and grace of a bull elk in the rutting season. Reaching the foot of the bed it began uttering muted but familiar oaths as it struggled manfully with knots in the half light. In a short while the heavy, gnarled fingers had succeeded in their task, and the sock was plucked from the bedpost. Still clutched by the dark, clandestine figure it was borne from the room, and along with it went the magic of Christmas.

So, against this background, it came as something of a surprise this Christmas morning to be confronted with an uncharacteristically bright and seasonal greeting from Father. "S'pose this be what y'do want is it?" he muttered dour faced, thrusting an already inflated football into my hands. I was temporarily speechless. I'd just recovered enough to begin thanking him effusively when I was cut short with,

"Tis a 'T' panel, best you can get. Look after it proper, an' if I catches you kickin' of em about on concrete or the road I'll give yer arse a warmin' y' won't forget!"

"What harm will that do to it?" I asked, chancing my arm a little.

"T'will scuff up the leather and bugger up the stitchin'. Then, when thees do 'ead 'un like professionals do, the rough leather 'll cut 'e fore'ead. I learned that when I did play for Portsmouth!"

Father never did play for Portsmouth. He had turned out once or twice for Cowplain in some obscure division of the Spithead and District league. But for all that, his advice seemed sound and worth heeding.

I was awoken on the following Saturday morning by the sound of a football bouncing repeatedly on concrete, and intermittently against something wooden. Pulling on my clothes as rapidly as possible I cantered down the stairs, out of the back door, across our yard, and into the cow yard. There I watched non plussed as, shoulders hunched, upper torso weaving in an intricate feint, Father launched upon a mazy dribble around at least half a dozen comparatively pedestrian cowpats.

At the far end of the yard, gloved hands spread, palms outwards in front of his chest, and legs bent in hairtrigger anticipation, stood Wally the displaced Pole, determinedly defending the cowshed door. Having nutmeged the final cowpat, cutting a deep swathe through its concentrically rippled surface, Father unleashed a thunderous right-footed shot. Trailing a spray of bovine effluent in its wake, the ball flew doorwards. Wally launched himself to his left and succeeded in parrying it into the cow trough.

Feeling an indignant little bristle coming on I strode over to where Father was fishing the ball out of the trough, and confronted him with his edict on using the ball on concrete.

"'S alright" he said dismissively. "Bugger me the concrete's damp;

t'won't do it any 'arm!"

As I walked away I felt bruised by a deep sense of injustice. 'Don't do as I do, do as I say!' seemed a very convenient maxim for adults to live by. It was no more or less than I'd come to expect of Father, but in Wally I felt disappointed. A stocky, taciturn Pole in his mid-thirties, with rugged, chiselled good looks, he was a victim of war-torn Europe, and was now classified as displaced, but he and I had formed a close friendship. His taciturnity was largely, I suspect, due to his inability to come to terms with the English language. He awkwardly spoke enough to get by, but Wally still thought, and dreamt, in Polish, and spoke often of going back.

What skills Wally lacked linguistically he more than made up for in his hands. He was forever carving me wooden toys. He made a superb catapult, and a set of pecking chickens, operated by a wooden weight and strings, but his *piece-de-resistance* was an exploding *Queen Mary*. The hull was some two feet long and carved out of the solid. The deck, superstructure, bridge, funnels, masts and rigging were all made separately and detached. Inside the hull he'd fitted a spring rat trap mechanism, and from this through to the outside ran a wooden stud. Depressing this stud released the mechanism, the arm of which threw the decks and other fittings high into the air, in a truly realistic 'explosion'.

Despite his limited grasp of English Wally was also a master story teller. Many's the lunch hour I've sat on a straw bale or sack of cow cake transfixed as he unwound some mysterious tale or other. But Wally suddenly disappeared. One morning he simply failed to turn up for work. A couple of days later Father's boss made enquiries at his lodgings in Westbury to be told that he'd paid up to date and, without as much as a by-your-leave, had left with no explanation or forwarding address. As far as I am aware, none of us ever heard of Wally again. His leaving had been as puzzling and mysterious as his lunch-time tales.

3.
Conkers, Hobnails and
a Yawning Abyss

IT WAS ABOUT THIS TIME that I really seemed to fall foul of Father's wrath at every turn. Boots were a subject of high contention. Most of the kids at school were, by now, wearing rubber-soled shoes but I, along with a few other youngsters from the less well-off homes in the village, was still turned out in hob-nails.

"I'm not throwin' good money away on thik flimsy rubbish, so as you can kick the guts out o' 'em in thik playground!" bellowed Father whenever the subject was broached.

It was about every three weeks or so that Father held his 'snobbing surgery'. Sat in front of the kitchen range, his last gripped between his knees, he'd set up a hollow resonant rhythm banging an assortment of studs, segs and quarter tips into the dampened leather soles.

"Thees cassn't kip these 'ere modern vulcanised rubbish on th' road wi' a few well 'ammered studs!" he'd observe pointedly.

He'd already treated the school to a taste of impromptu theatre when responding to the Headmistress's letter circularized to all parents of hobnail wearing pupils. As tactfully as possible it had begged them to appreciate the damage caused by studded soles to the cross-stretchers of the new school desks, and asked them to consider the merits of rubber-soled footwear. Father viewed it as a dictate to his freedom of choice and in consequence had stormed unannounced into the school one morning and confronted Mrs Sheppard in front of her class. Having just driven his milking herd to a field beyond the school, he hovered over her, a picture of self-righteous indignation, cowshit all over his boots and still clutching his sturdy hazel cowstick which Mrs Sheppard eyed nervously.

"Second class citizens thats 'ow you'm treatin' 'em!" Father ranted accusingly. "Picked on at every turn my boy is!" he continued, wagging a rather unsavoury finger vigorously under her nose. Mrs Sheppard's colour had moved a few shades down through the spectrum, but she held herself together valiantly and ushered Father out into an anti-room, much to the disappointment of the class who were by now eagerly looking forward to fur flying. Left unattended the class broke into pandemonium. Miss Rutledge, her assistant, burst in from the adjoining classroom just as the hail of ink pellets, paper planes and coloured chalks was at its thickest, and the carnival atmosphere was killed at a stroke.

What had coloured Father's response to the letter was, in essence, 'the big ship going through the Alley-Alley-O', and the partial eclipse of the sun. A couple of weeks earlier a few other hobnail-shod lads and myself were engaged in a serious game of sliding. When hobnail boots are used on smooth tarmac you carry your very own ice-rink.

Now 'sliding' had been strictly outlawed by Mrs Sheppard as it was deemed dangerous to other pupils. But no matter, we still slid, and the distances were slowly improving. Going for the big-one, I surpassed the previous mark by some considerable distance, and collided with the snake of kids engaged in playing 'The big ship goes through the Alley-Alley-O'. In a tangle of arms and legs we sprawled on the floor. One of the last up was the blubbing figure of stupid Myrtle Biggs. Not having the wit to break her own fall she was now sporting angry looking grazes to her hand, elbow and cheek. My heart sank, the way it has a habit of doing when the high jump is seen looming and you know instinctively that you're the one for it.

Sure enough, positively identified by soppy Myrtle, I was hauled before Mrs Sheppard. Severely dressed down, I was told that for the next fortnight my playtimes and lunchbreaks would be spent sitting in the classroom repetitively scribbling 'Playgrounds were not made for sliding in!'

It so happened that this fortnight of incarceration was set to coincide with an event of such spell-binding magnitude that even Mrs Sheppard might need a hand to pull it off. The predicted partial eclipse of the sun had fermented a great air of expectancy in the school. A ping-pong ball, an orange and a swede were suspended on strings and referred to *ad nauseam* as the planetary interplay was drummed into us. The moon's path was plotted with a broken chalk line on the blackboard until we had imbibed it chapter and verse. The afternoon before the great obfuscation we were all instructed to bring with us the following day either glass or celluloid photographic negatives through which we could observe the event without dam-

34

aging our eyes.

That evening I approached Father with the request for a negative. "It's so we can watch the eclipse without burning our eyes!" I informed him.

"Eclipse?" he queried, "the only clips I knows about stops me trouser bottoms from flappin' in the back wheel o' me bike!" He, of course, was joking I think! "S'don't want no negatives. The best way to look at bright lights is drew a piece o' smoked glass!" So saying he disappeared out into the shed, returning a short while later with a small rectangular sheet of glass, a tin lid and a tin of oil. He set the tin lid down on the hearth and then, importuning a large piece of cloth from Mother, he placed this in the tin lid and doused it in oil. When lit, the rag gave off a thick black smoke. Father, holding the glass above it, twisted it so that both sides were covered in a thick sooty deposit. Satisfied at last, and about thirty seconds before we all died of asphyxia, he stifled the blaze. Taking a sheet of cardboard, he folded it double, cutting a window in both sections. He then inserted the sheet of smoked glass into its protective frame.

"There," he said, looking very full of himself, "That's better than all yer bloody negatives! Make sure thee don't touch the surface an rub thik soot off," he instructed, sliding it into a paper bag for further protection, "Otherwise 'twill be wuss than useless!".

So, armed with my innovative sunshield, I arrived at school the next day full of high spirits, but those spirits soon came spiralling down as I learned that there was to be no relaxing of my fortnight's detention; so the lunchtime break in which the eclipse would occur would be spent in the confines of the classroom.

I could hear the excited chatter of my classmates in the yard and the strident tones of Mrs Sheppard instructing their observations. I abandoned writing 'Playgrounds are not made' etc. for what seemed like the thirty-sixth millionth time and, leaving the desk, manoeuvred my way over to the window to try and catch a glimpse of the spectacle, but the north facing window was yielding nothing. It was just at that moment I became involved in a partial eclipse of my very own. Or at least the object that had entered the room had the girth and volume of a medium-sized asteroid.

"What are you doing out of your seat? Detention isn't for playing games you know!" barked Miss Rutledge.

"I was trying to see the eclipse!" I replied sheepishly.

"Well you should have though of that before you went crashing into Myrtle Biggs," she continued caustically. Miss Rutledge could best be described as ample, very ample! Some might describe her as ugly, but that's because she was. This deficiency she attempted to hide with large quantities of powder and paint. But Battersea Power Station, painted and decorated by Botticelli, for all his fine endeavours, would still remain Battersea Power Station.

On this particular day Miss Rutledge had chosen to wear a voluminous floral patterned summer dress, with stiff lapels and sporting an improprietously plunging neckline. By now, I was sat back in my chair with Miss Rutledge bringing her face down to my level to make some edifying point or other. Her words did not register, as my senses were overwhelmed by a pungent, cloyingly sweet odour. It seemed to be issuing from somewhere in the region of the improprietous neckline. I found myself staring straight down the yawning abyss of Miss Rutledge's cleavage. Two mighty mole-pocked mammaries fought each other desperately as they strained to disinter themselves from constraining raiments, and somewhere in the far distance her voice droned on.

It would be at least a couple of years yet before I began to realise the sexual significance of the panorama set before me. But to this day I have only to catch whiff of a musky, pungent scent to see the spectre of Miss Rutledge's heaving decolletage swimming in a pink mist before my eyes.

Father was a little less than pleased to be told that his ingenious smoked glass viewer had gone unused.

"What a bloody waste of time!" he reacted. "They've no soddin' right to stop you seein' summat like that. Part o' yer edjicashun that is!"

So incensed was he, and so filled with a sense of injustice, I almost feared that to ensure I did witness my partial eclipse of the sun he might just be moved to send me to school the following morning with a patch over one eye.

It was around this time that I found myself reacting to many factors by cheating whenever I could. The royal and ancient game of 'conkers' gave me admirable scope for bending the rules.

Wally, the displaced Pole, had tutored me fairly soundly in the preparation of conkers. Always choose large, well ripened and round specimens. Steep in vinegar for about five days. Roast very slowly in a gentle heat, then rub dubbin into the hardened shell to restore elasticity. Always bore holes with brace and bit, never with a skewer, which expands the flesh causing tiny fissures which expand into cracks during play. Always use a soft lace and a very large knot. Never harsh string that cuts into the conker's flesh, or a small knot that pulls through.

Armed with all these tips I had a good head start on the other tactically more naive kids, and my success rate reflected this. However, it seemed that this wasn't enough and I soon expanded on the rules. When two conkers fail to connect cleanly the result is often a tangle of strings, and by tradition he who first shouts 'stringseez!' gets a free hit. It was this rule that I expanded upon.

'*Stringseez!*'

Having first shouted 'stringseez!' my gullible opponent gleefully relaxed his grip to disentangle the strings. At the very moment his defences were down, a sharp yank on the string wrenched the conker from his grasp and sent it careering across the playground. Invoking my brand new rule 37B, this was the moment I yelled 'stampseez'. He could only watch in open-mouthed disbelief as I caught up with his coveted 63'er and brought the full weight of my foot down to deliver the *coup-de-grace*. No matter how well prepared the conker, in head to head combat with the sole of a well directed hobnail boot, there is but one outcome.

Without doubt however, my greatest deception at that time, and the one that in later life caused me the most shame was at the wall. The wall in question was at the back of the boys' urinal trough. Above this trough gouged with penknives, or shakily written in pencil, were lines at varying heights, accompanied by names and dates. The dates only went back to 1948 when the toilets were redecorated, but even so there were some illustrious names recorded there.

On May 12th that year one John Parfitt had established the benchmark by jetting a little golden stream some four feet six inches up the wall. In October of the same year Ronald Platt stole the record by projecting his little offering about two inches higher. April 23rd the following year saw Ernie Fosset increased the standard by an incredible six inches. This stood until March 1950 when Mark Smith, having probably consumed a whole bottle of Dandelion and Burdock, increased it by the odd inch, only to see it snatched back again a month later by the irrepressible Ernie Fosset. And so the role of greats continued with Davey Clements, Davey Clements again, Mike Burgess, Len Piggford, Barry Thomas, Freddie Apps, Marjorie Landsbury (a bit suspect that one), Graham Garrett, and sitting at the top of the pile since September 29th 1952, Andy Sims.

Well I tried, I sat cross-legged through morning lessons till I was plum in the face, stood on tip toe, arched my back, clenched my buttocks together, coughed and took a run at it – but all to no avail. At my best I was still a good eighteen inches short. I desperately wanted my name on that wall above Andy Sims, but Winter was fast approaching, and you know what winter can do to record attempts of that nature. So I hatched a cunning ploy. Secreted in my trouser pocked, along with a penknife, a piece of knotted string, sundry conker shards, three dead woodlice, and a very interesting piece of rubbery substance I'd found adhering to the Post Office railings, was a small water-pistol, about three inches long with a water containing rubber bulb for a handle.

I stood at the trough with two of my peers, one vainly trying to attain altitude, one acting more modestly. I waited until sundry shaking and tucking was completed and they'd just disappeared out of the door before producing my pistol and aiming a jet up the wall. I was tempted to go all the way to the top and command eternal veneration, but thought it would be wiser to appear more plausible and just top Andy Sims mark by a couple of inches. The deed done,

I raced out of the door and grabbed the pair, who a moment before had been at the trough with me. Propelling them inside I invited them to witness the telltale wet stain that darkened the wall.

With expressions of disbelief and awe they gawped at the evidence, before running from the toilet shouting,

"He's done it. Toby's topped the mark!" Within seconds at least a dozen snotty noses appeared round the door, and congratulations were showered upon me. Had I climbed Everest with both feet tied together and a comatosed water buffalo strapped to my back their adulation could scarcely have been greater. The bona fides of the attempt were never questioned. The playground dustbin was hauled in, and a stubby red pencil produced from the depths of Caggy Walsh's trouser pocket. I clambered up and purposefully scrawled the inscription – 'TOBY DYER OCTOBER 10th 1953'.

In the years that have followed I have often felt pangs of guilt at such wanton deception. But none so strong that I have been moved to take column inches in the local press to apologise to the duped.

4.
Leg-spinners, Retribution and Marrow Rum

THE SOUND OF LEATHER on willow echoing from those halcyon village greens has long seduced the bucolic bard to wax lyrical. Less so the sound of leather on juvenile buttocks.

Despite often living within proverbial spitting distance of a village green it was, of the two, the latter that was most commonly encountered in our household. Father's disciplinary methods were simple, arbitrary and very much of the belt and buckle variety. There was 'bed with no supper', the belt, or perhaps, on vintage days, the belt and to bed with no supper. Such retribution was normally meted out at the behest of Mother.

As Father arrived home from a hard day's toil, exuding his customary dearth of bonhomie, she'd waylay him at the door and bleat piteously,

"He's been at it again Frank, and I'm at my wits end!" Sparing no more than a rudimentary grunt of acknowledgement he would confront me, unbuckling his belt.

Now Father's belt should not be pictured as one of those wimpish devices designed for holding up trousers. He had a pair of elasticated braces to perform that menial task. No, his belt was the type used more as a lumbar support, and for hauling tractors out of ditches. A good three inches wide it was, and as thick as a bookie's wallet. It was fastened by a huge, heavy brass buckle, no doubt purloined at some stage from a plough horse's harness. Long experience had taught me what to expect as he doubled it and pulled it taut, causing both halves to crack sharply together. Any protestations of innocence, or pleas for lenience on my part fell upon deaf ears, as he resolutely set about his task. There was never, as I recall, any suggestion of malevolence or sadism behind his actions. More, I think, he viewed it all in a recreational light. The perfect way to unwind after a hard day's work.

Nursing an injured pride and an inflamed behind I often heard Father inquiring, as he washed his hands and allowed his heart-beat to return to normal, exactly what misdemeanour Mother considered had warranted his correction.

"Well bugger me!" he'd often respond, "Thee's could've laid down the law to un theeself. Thee dussn't have t' wait fer I t' come 'ome an' gi'un a leatherin'. Twasn't worth a good 'idin' anyhow". For all that, I never did receive an apology for a thrashing unjustly administered. Nor – and this rankled far more deeply – did I ever receive a credit note for the next one.

Father was a keen vegetable gardener, and it was as a result of this that I received some of my most severe leatherings. 'Bowling' was one activity I recall that put the well-being of my backside in jeopardy. I'd chalked a set of cricket stumps on the back door and was busily emulating Eric Bedser. Then, with a slight adjustment of fingers on the ball, I became Jim Laker. I'd just got line and length on a patch of rough that was causing the ball to break back viciously when the wickets suddenly disappeared. Mother stood at the open door.

"Take that bloody ball somewhere else," she wailed. "Dap, dap, dap, that's all I can hear, it's driving me bats!"

Foolishly I ignored her, and, lengthening my run up considerably, I became Typhoon Tyson. Generating awesome speed, and still profiting from the patch of rough, my deliveries were cutting a swathe through the Australian middle order when, just two balls into my fourth over, the wickets suddenly disappeared once more.

"Right that's it" squealed Mother. "Just wait till your bloody Father gets home that's all!"

Those words cast a pall of gloom over the rest of the day, and sure enough teatime saw a tattoo of retribution beaten out on my backside. Buckling his belt back on, Father had the good grace to enquire of Mother,

"What the hell's he been up to now?"

"Dapping a bloody ball on the door all afternoon that's what, proper got on my fittin's!" replied Mother defensively."

"Don't s'pose 'twould 'ave been easier to take the ball away from 'un?" he queried.

Mother declined to reply. For once I felt that the injustice of my punishment was making inroads into Father's conscience. But not for long. Within the hour he was unbuckling his belt again, this time in a steaming black rage. Wandering out to tend his vegetable patch he'd discovered that Frank Tyson's extended run up had cut right across the corner of his seed bed.

If violation of a seed bed warranted a good beating, what price the partial destruction of two rows of main crop peas? Hell fire, damnation and a scourging of the utmost severity would look about par for the course. So it proved. With nostrils distended and small blue veins standing out on his temples Father wielded his belt with demonic fervour. Added to which there would be no tea to lend solace to my throbbing nethers, or to my injured pride. Not tonight, nor for the next two nights.

It was the injustice of it all that stuck so painfully in my craw. After all, had I not been the good guy? It was Caggy Walsh, Whip Wellings and Les Clutterbuck who were the German Stormtroopers. By sheer weight of numbers they had forced me, the solitary, clean-cut, square-jawed British Marine Commando, to make my final defiant stand between the two rows of peas. All would have been well if they had contented themselves by keeping me pinned down with the withering fusilade of rifle and machine gun impressions coming from behind the rhubarb. But no, grabbed by a foolish wave of bravado, and lobbing a number of Father's beetroots as grenades, Caggy led the ill-fated bayonet charge. It was not Caggy himself who was first to crash headlong through the peas, for he had slipped and lay spreadeagled amongst the cos lettuce, but educationally subnormal Les Clutterbuck – he of the platelike feet and permanently puzzled expression. Now Les might not have been a radiant beacon in the field of education, but my God, he couldn't half destroy a row of peas!

Before I could open my mouth to remonstrate, Whip Wellings, confusing both the conflict and the continent, hurtled through after him yelling 'Geronimo!!'. Ricocheting off the bewildered Les, he careered straight through the second row of peas. Almost simultaneously Les let out a yell of anguish as a beetroot, lobbed by Caggy – now spitting fragments of lettuce and regaining his feet – connected squarely with the back of his head

"Right, surrender! " demanded Caggy. "We've got y' covered!"

There was little point in surrendering. I instinctively knew that the moment Father got home, I was a dead man. Considering the mayhem caused I don't suppose his fury was too unjustified. He was, after all, an avid gardener. Most of his spare time, not spent at the pub, was invested in his garden. He never had time for flowers. 'Pretty blooms won't feed thee!' he used to remark. But his vegetables were tended with an almost pedantic enthusiasm. Crouching down, squinting along his row of cabbage plants, he'd suddenly straighten and rolling his dog-end along his bottom lip with dextrous tongue, exclaim,

"Buggered if I ain't going to 'ave to move they four in the middle back a smidgen, they baint suant!"

So saying, the offending plants were carefully relocated so that they were 'suant' (straight and orderly) across the plot like parading guardsmen.

His forte was producing vegetables to enter in local village shows. Over the years he won many classes. He was noted for being a smug braggart in victory and far from magnanimous in defeat. Such was his reputation that the hapless individuals whose misfortune it had been to judge the sections in which Father was competing kept a weather eye open for his approach, had his exhibit been less than triumphant.

"What's wrong wi 'um, you tell me that!" I heard Father's irate voice demanding from the far end of the produce marquee. "Bloody zite bigger than them I 'low!" he challenged as I wormed my way through a rapidly gathering crowd.

I found him waving an onion intimidatingly under the nose of an elderly, sallow-faced man with a small blue cardboard shield dangling from his lapel proclaiming 'Official' in gold lettering. It was Mr Latcham the semi-retired proprietor of a well known local animal feed and farm seed suppliers.

The show committee had voted to honour Mr Latcham by asking him to judge the vegetable section of the show. I was witnessing the moment when that honour was turning sour. Confronted by an abnormally large fist, clutching an abnormally large onion to which he had only seen fit to give a highly commended award, Mr Latcham's prominent Adam's apple bobbed up and down convulsively as his ashen face took on the look of an injured rabbit cornered by a particularly rapacious ferret. It was all too obvious that at this very moment he was wishing that he could be separated from the small dangling blue shield by at least the length of the Pennine Way.

To his eternal credit Mr Latcham stood his ground, and setting frail shoulders and quivering chin he replied,

"The five onions were judged on shape and uniformity not just on size!"

"Shape and uniformity?" bellowed Father as Mr Latcham's fragile assertiveness disintegrated. "I've been enterin' these shows fer nigh on twenty years, so don't try tellin' me 'ow they're judged. Tis size thee's do want. Bugger me, thee's cassn't eat shape and uniformity'. An' what about the longest runner bean, measured be a blind man were it? Mine were a good dree inches longer than old Fenwick's!"

"But with a number of bad imperfections!" offered the browbeaten Mr Latcham hopefully.

"Didn't say a soddin' thing about imperfections on the entry form!" roared Father, obviously playing to the crowd.

By now, looking lurcher-backed and forlorn, old Mr Latcham declined to fight his corner any longer. Turning, he walked away with as much dignity as he could muster, Father's voice still ringing in his ears.

"And I suppose my parsnips 'ad a number of bad imperfections too!" he mocked. "That told the know-all bugger," he said, turning to the assembled onlookers for approbation. Acute embarrassment flooded through me as I dissolved quietly from the tent.

If Father's belligerent attitude had created discomfiture at village shows, then his vegetable marrows had, over the years, caused much consternation at cottage hospitals. He did produce some amazing examples. Nourished by liquid manure and dried blood, his one selected specimen was lovingly nurtured until it lay amongst the foliage like an enormous grounded Zeppelin. Twenty-eight pounders were not unknown and, in some misplaced annual surge of public spiritedness he would, each Autumn, present one of these massive, fleshy gourds to a local hospital. Being too polite to refuse, they were then saddled with the problem of what to do with it. Just exactly what do you do with a twenty-eight pound marrow?

That question having been posed, it was answered one year by Father himself, albeit with a marrow of slightly more modest tonnage. Marrow rum had been mentioned down at the White Lion, and he was all ears.

"Apparently," said Father, inspecting the specimen marrow laying on the kitchen table with a glow of considerable satisfaction, "All y' does is cut off the top, scoop out the seeds, fill 'n wi' brown sugar and make a hole in the bottom. Then thee's do 'ang 'n up in a bit o' mutton cloth an let 'n drip into a bottle"

"I don't know!" ventured Mother, "You sure it's alright. I mean you do hear o' these people goin' blind drinkin' 'ome made spirits!"

"Not wi' marrow rum you don't!" countered Father exasperatedly. "Has thee got arn bit o' mutton cloth 'angin' about?" A rather stained piece was rummaged from a drawer, and he set about disemboweling the marrow. A few minutes later, stuffed with brown sugar and suspended in its muslin cradle, the marrow was borne up two flights of stairs to the attic. There it was hung on a nail in one of the exposed beams, suspended over a bottle with a funnel in it.

The marrow was borne up two flights of stairs to the attic.

"I reckons that'll serve up a fair drop of jollop for Christmas," said Father contemplatively stroking the wiry stubble of his chin. The attic door creaked shut, and the marrow was forgotten for about five weeks.

Mother was in the kitchen one evening having taken to a hammer and cold chisel in an attempt to dislodge six fairy cakes that flatly refused to budge from their baking tray. Father, slouched in his favourite armchair, absently prodded the poker into a couple of sycamore logs on the fire and bemoaned the fact that he couldn't afford a trip down the pub. Suddenly, the very fabric of the house was shaken by the dull thud of an explosion.

"Bugger me!" exclaimed Father, sitting bolt upright in his chair, and leaving the poker wedged in the fire. "Sounded like a bloody girt bomb that did!" A quick sortee to the back door revealed nothing.

"Could have been a car back-firing!" offered Mother helpfully.

"No, too muffled a bang for that!" observed Father, "Still, bloody queer though for all that!"

Wearing a bemused frown he sank back heavily into his chair, but was galvanised in an instant with a yell of 'Jesus!' as he grasped the poker which by now had heated up considerably.

Two days later, Mother was cleaning the bedroom when she discovered a sticky deposit adhering to the bedside mat. On the ceiling, directly above, she noticed a large, brown, damp patch. Clambering up the attic stairs and opening the door brought her face to face with total havoc. Lumps of dried marrow clung tenaciously to every surface. A thick brown syrup oozed at a snail's pace down the walls. Tiny pendant stalactites hung from the ceiling. The tattered remnants of the mutton cloth cradle hung forlornly from the nail, but the funnel and bottle lay on the floor having leaked the precious contents discovered in the bedroom below. The fermentation process had obviously got well out of hand and blown Father's little rum factory to smithereens. When he arrived home from work, Mother propelled him urgently up the stairs. Confronted by scenes of utter devastation he reacted with,

"What a bloody shame, looks like that would 'ave been a main powerful drop o' stuff!"

5.
Coronations, Winkles & Dunghampers

1953 HAD PROVED TO BE a pretty middling sort of year for Father so far. It had started with the loss of Ginge, his favourite cat. Run over by an egg distribution van. Shortly after that his boss had paid a snap visit expecting to find him and old Will Painter in the barn, utilising a wet day, making spars for rick thatching. Instead, they were discovered having a crafty fag and a hand of 'pontoon'. Father's normal defensive reaction to being caught out would have been to explode on the spot, issuing advice in no uncertain terms as to the exact anatomical location for the insertion of his job. But, crass as he was, he still recognised when he'd landed on his feet. His first bailiff's post had brought him a greatly improved wage and, at last, some reasonable accommodation. So, with uncharacteristic self restraint, he apologetically wormed and fawned his way out of the situation. The curbing of his basic Neanderthal instincts, however, had left a bitter taste and he lapsed into a mood that was, for some time, even more surly and morose than usual.

On the strength of his improved wage, he had even seen fit to boast to his cronies in the pub that he'd have a television in to watch the Coronation, only to be forced to eat humble pie when he discovered that they were still well beyond what he could afford. This general downturn in fortunes hadn't been at all improved by Scroggie. Scroggie had been found as an infant by Wally the displaced Pole. Red squirrels were a rarity even in those days and this little chap, it appeared, had either been orphaned or simply mislaid by his parents, as he was discovered bewildered and very vulnerable on the woodland floor. He was taken into the family fold and suckled on the corner of a handkerchief steeped in a milk and sugar mixture. He thrived and as he grew Father thought it would be a great idea to teach him tricks. Scroggie didn't! He rejected all of Father's painstaking tuition out of hand, disdainfully introducing a range of his own tricks. Stolen toffees were wedged behind pictures and curtain rails. Dog ends, stolen from behind Father's ear, were rammed down the back of the settee. Buttons were plucked from Mother's button box and buried in the geranium pots, all except the red ones which were, for some mysterious reason, invariably dropped into the goldfish bowl. But, without doubt, his favourite jape, always carried out with a self-satisfied smirk wreathing his impish chops, was to bounce both front feet down on the handle of the spoon resting in the sugar bowl and watch a shower of white granules catapult into the air. Exhausted by his endeavours, he normally retired to an armchair and curled up with one of the cats for a recuperative snooze, rebounding a short while later with yet more mischievous intent.

A shower of white granules catapult into the air.

His disruptive antics weren't confined to the house alone. He often made excursions out into the farm buildings or over into next door's garden where he was revered by both farm hands and neighbours alike, for his puckish sense of fun. It wasn't these factors by themselves which added to Father's woes, but one isolated incident stemming from Scroggie's peregrinations. Mrs Parsons, our next door neighbour, was a kindly soul who had a very soft spot for Scroggie. She always kept little scraps of kipper to one side, knowing this was his particular weakness. She was a very large lady. Not unlike my teacher, Miss Rutledge, in general bulk but built much more along stout yeoman lines. She lacked the soft, puffy flesh and elevated bosom of Miss Rutledge. No airs and graces here, but good sturdy forearms and broad shoulders supporting a neck like a prize Charolais bull. She had ruddy, weathered features and greying hair strained back into a bun. Father maintained that she'd developed her oxen build in the early years of her marriage, helping her husband with the ploughing, during the hard times, before they could afford a horse.

My first inkling that all was not well came with the sound of Father's voice wafting in from the garden. It carried with it a strange quality, sounding as though he was attempting to be reassuring and yet seized by an underlying panic. Quite quickly the reassuring element subsided, as the panic escalated. He began to holler Mother's name,

"Gwen! Gwen," he yelled, "For Christ's sake come out here."

There was no disguising the tone in the voice now – it was one of unconcealed desperation.

I followed Mother along the passage and out into the garden. I couldn't believe what I was seeing. Father was not in our garden, but in next doors, performing some strange dance with Mrs Parsons. With a backcloth of washing flapping in the breeze, she was jigging her great bulk up and down on one leg, whilst thrashing the other around in the air like a demented Can Can girl. Although she wore a skirt of the utmost modesty her wild tarantella was intermittantly revealing a very voluminous pair of pink flannel drawers, elasticated at the knee. All the while Father was cautiously circling in a semi-crouched position, every so often tentatively extending an open hand towards Mrs Parsons hemline and then withdrawing it as though bitten by an adder.

"Well don't just stand there woman, do something!" he chided Mother. His face had lost much of its customary colour and his eyes were those of a field mouse menaced by a stoat.

"Summats frightened the 'ell out o' Scroggie, an' 'es shot up 'er skirts!" he panted, "He's still up thur a clingin' to 'er dunghampers.

I can't just go thrustin' me 'and up thur after 'un!'"

At that moment Mrs Parsons toppled backwards, tripping over her washing basket. As this terpsichoreal leviathan crashed to the ground both her legs went up in the air exposing the full acreage of her flannel drawers. Scroggie, in even greater fear of his life, bolted headlong from the floundering mass. Seconds later he was sat in the uppermost branches of a damson tree, chuntering and flicking his russet brush in self-righteous indignation. Father flapped helplessly around Mrs Parsons as she struggled unsteadily to her feet, before taking his leave and clambering back over the garden fence. He fumbled urgently in his jacket pocket for his baccy tin, desperately needing the solace of a roll-up. Staring back down the garden he could see the extensive figure of Mrs Parsons lightly dabbing the perspiration from her forehead with a vest she'd hauled from the washing basket. As he brought the lighted match to his roll-up, his hand trembled.

All this, and now, with Coronation celebrations less than a fortnight away, further ill-fortune had swooped on Father like a black raven of doom. The centrepiece of the village celebrations was to be the sports day and fancy dress parade in the field behind the school. Much to my distaste Mother had entered me in the fancy dress, the theme of which was to be British History. My trepidation at the prospect of being turned out like a total prat was eased only slightly by the knowledge that some of my school chums had been cornered by their parents too.

Caggy Walsh had misguidedly been practicing hopping on one leg for a fortnight to lend authenticity to his role as Horatio Nelson. It had taken half the bed linen in the house to get Smelly Drinkwater dressed up as Lawrence of Arabia. Andy Sims had fallen victim to his parents whimsical sense of humour. Carrying a poker, a pair of fire tongs and a trivet, with his head surrounded by a halo of cardboard flames, he was reluctantly going as 'Alfred the Grate'.

We'd sounded out a couple of Robin Hoods and a Charlie Chaplin. We'd also worked out that the insufferable, school 'golden boy' Jerome Leatherwood, who boasted wearing the same brand of shoes as Prince Charles, and also had an acute bladder problem, would probably turn up as 'Ethelred the Incontinent'. By using coercion, and threatening to strangle her with her own licorice bootlace, we'd succeeded in forcing gormless Myrtle Biggs into revealing that she would be appearing as Florence Nightingale. Whilst her equally appalling friend Marjorie Wheeler was lending her freckles and suppurating cold sores to the role of Mary Queen of Scots.

Even camouflaged by this motley back-up I was still uneasy about going public. True, Mother had done a fine job on my striped, puffy breeches, and had tailored a snappy little doublet. Father had chipped in with a wooden sword and stitched some harness buckles to my boots. And didn't I just look Jack the Lad with my green felt hat, with the wood pigeon feathers in it, worn at a rakish angle? But still somehow I was far from convinced that Sir Walter Raleigh had ever sailed the oceans of the world wearing a pair of my Mother's cast-off stockings.

It was the ruff worn at my neck that was causing Mother consternation this Sunday afternoon. Try as she might, she just could not get it to lay right. Inserting a length of cord one way, then the other, she resorted to a few choice expletives as each effort resulted in failure. Suddenly, and without warning, her cosy little suite of expletives was dramatically upstaged. Father was at the back door and approaching fast.

"Bugger, hellfire and damnation!" he stormed as he hove into view. He had been doing the afternoon's milking, and was clad in his white milking smock – or at least three sides of him were!

The front had been white once, but was now that special shade of green that enables infantrymen and army three-tonners to become totally invisible in mixed woodland. The diagnosis was simple: Father was suffering from 'Spring Grass Syndrome'. As it happened the herd had just been turned onto lush, fresh pasture. Now verdant spring grass improves not only the milk yield but also the flowing properties of certain bovine by-products. It was common practice at this time to record individual milk yield on a chart. Such a chart was hanging on the back wall of the cowshed, and Father had just made an entry upon it. He had the gross misfortune to turn back and face the cows just as one particularly smitten individual, contentedly evacuating her bowels, coughed violently. A fetid deluge of abnormally low viscosity was propelled with great force straight into his chest. There was no doubt about it – Father's karma was going through a distinctly lean spell.

Added to all this he was sorely regretting opening his big mouth at the recent village hall meeting. A suggestion had been put forward from the floor that it might be great fun to stage a tug-o-war contest between Heywood and the neighbouring village of Hawkridge as part of the Coronation day celebrations.

Amid the discussion, Father was overheard to remark upon his experiences in 1928, when the *H.M.S. Resource* had steamed into Valetta harbour, and he had been part of the ship's tug-o-war team that had taken on, and beaten, a motley assortment of limp-wristed Maltese gigolos. Too late he realized the error of sounding his own trumpet. He was swept up in the maelstrom, proposed, seconded and unanimously elected as captain, manager, coach and spiritual mentor of the Heywood tug-o-war team. This saddled him with the unenviable task of finding eight good men and true. It was surprising just how many of the local menfolk were otherwise committed. A plethora of holidays, in such tranquil suntraps as Bude, Eastbourne and Budleigh Salterton were suddenly conjured out of thin air. Hitherto perfectly fit, able-bodied individuals were seen to hobble pitiably at Father's approach. There seemed to be an unaccountable spate of sprains, strains and kidney disorders.

Eventually, through dogged perseverance he did manage to cobble together a team of sorts, but as it was comprised mostly of individuals lacking the wit to come up with a plausible excuse, the venture held out very little promise. Of the eight, only Father and Roly Betteridge seemed to possess the physical attributes necessary for the challenge. Roly was approximately five feet ten inches, whichever way you measured him. Of florid complexion, thin, straw-like fair hair and a rolling duck-like gait. He was a cheerful, affable character in his late thirties who, when passing a courteous time of day, would invariably append it with, 'Lookin' brighter over Wills' Mother's again'. No one ever discovered who Will or his Mother might be, nor indeed the location of the latter's residence. However, it was always somehow reassuring that we could thank them for any upturn in the weather. Apart from a few odd jobs, Roly never seemed to work, but always had enough money by him to stand his round down the pub, and consequently he was a popular local figure. He wasn't too bright and possessed a very slow wit which he would lamely camouflage by replying to everything said to him with 'Aha, I saw thik one comin'!' and then proceeding to laugh like a drain.

Had the communal budget been able to stretch to such luxuries he would certainly have taken on the role of official village idiot. But for all that, Roly had his uses. He may have been corpulent, slow and ponderous but, when he was dug in, he took an awful lot of shifting. Mind you, once toppled and rolling he was unstoppable. So here was the team's anchor man.

Father made sure that the whole team had kitted themselves out with a good sturdy pair of army-type boots, and then assembled them for a spot of coaching. Being keen to see how the big boy splayed I went to watch. Father had driven the farm's trusty Standard Fordson tractor out into home ground and attached a rope to the front axle. With the team in position he released the brake and knocked it out of gear, quickly joining them, in an attempt to see how far they could haul it up a slight incline.

"Heave," shouted Father, "Heave! Right now, hold. Heave!"

Steel-tipped heels cut deeply into the yielding turf, and grunts of exertion arose from seven straining bodies leaning at 20° to the ground. The eighth, Roly, was still pretty much upright and looking confused. It had already taken him more that a quarter of an hour to grasp the principles of winding the rope over the shoulder, under the arm and round his waist to obtain an anchorman's grip. With sweat now pouring, the other seven strained determinedly on the rope. With the final command of 'Hold!' Father strode back to the tractor to see just how far they'd hauled it. He began to realize just how much work still had to be done when he discovered that it had actually slipped back a couple of feet.

To everyone's obvious relief the day of the Coronation celebration sports and fancy dress dawned bright and virtually cloudless. This was far from my outlook on life as I viewed myself in the mirror. I looked an utter pillock. I was never cut out to be Sir Walter Raleigh and I couldn't for the life of me understand why he had to get togged up like this just to build bicycles. Mother was engrossed, crayoning on my beard and moustache, but I was deeply conscious that one of my stockings was laddered.

"Oh my God!" I thought, "If Avril Pearce sees me like this, she'll never share her sherbert dab with me again!"

Still wishing that I could crawl into a hedge and whimper, I was dragged into the sports field. The usual assortment of stalls dotted the periphery of the ground. A large beer tent had been erected, and next to it three sheets of hessian surrounded a hastily dug trench. Hundreds of flies, having quickly deduced that this would be used as the latrines, were already heading in that general direction. Tarpaulins, car tyres hung on wooden frames and large wooden barrels were already in position for the obstacle race. A large wooden pole was suspended horizontally over an artificial pool of water contained in a tarpaulin. The board next to it read 'Jousting Lake 2d.' Bunting and Union Jacks flapped everywhere in the breeze, and I felt desolate. I bucked up a little however when I spotted Caggy. He was looking as comprehensive a prawn as I was. So, for that matter, was Smelly Drinkwater. His portrayal of Lawrence of Arabia, with a snotty nose and a pair of unpolished hobnail boots sticking out from under an ill-draped bed sheet, was far from convincing.

We were all lined up by Mrs Sheppard, in no particular order it seemed, as I was between Jerome Leatherwood and the Laycock twins. Jerome's incredibly rich parents had spared no expense in turning him out as Charles I. I don't know where they got the ostrich plumes for his hat, but they made my wood pigeon feathers look quite rural. Chris and Graham, the Laycock twins, were imaginatively got up as St. George and the Dragon. Chris wore some very authentic cardboard and foil armour, but the effect was somewhat undermined when we came to Graham, whose cardboard dragon costume was already beginning to fall apart at the seams. I could just see his eyes peering out through the mouth, and he looked decidedly uncomfortable in there, struggling to hold it all together. It was a very poorly made effort. It didn't look very much like the popular image of a dragon and, apart from the colour, reminded one more of a rather ill-tempered dachshund. The coat of red paint had been too thinly applied to the cardboard body, and over its entire surface such wording as 'Weetabix', 'Oxydol-washes vivid white' and 'Huntley and Palmers' could be clearly read.

The judging was being done by Mrs Aspinwall, wife of the local landowner, and a J.P in her own right. What we had not been prepared for was her asking testing questions about the characters we were portraying. Caggy panicked, and said he thought Nelson was a pirate who had hidden his treasure from the Spanish Armada at Waterloo. Dozy Myrtle had gawped thunderstruck, and eventually wet herself. But of course smarty-arsed Jerome, next to me, had come up with at least a dozen rivetting facts about Charles I, whilst I was at a complete loss for facts about Sir Walter bloody Raleigh, other than that he was probably some med-ieval raver who went round in women's stockings. It was poor old Graham I felt sorry for, sweating away inside his cardboard dachshund. Bowing an immaculately coiffured head towards him, Mrs Aspinwall asked what he knew about dragons. As he laboured to find an answer, his lower left arm, clearly bearing the legend 'Spratts Mixed Ovals' fell to the ground.

About half an hour passed before the result was announced. When it was, there was uproar, and Father was in the middle of it. I came nowhere. Caggy had done somewhat better than expected by also coming nowhere, but Smelly Drinkwater had surpassed all expectations by coming just behind us. Myrtle Biggs had gone into the school cloakroom to change her underwear, and the insufferable Jerome Leatherwood had been announced as runner up. But it was the announcement of the winner that stirred up the furore.

"And the worthy winner," fawned Mr Willett, local Councillor and show organiser, "is Cicely Givens as the Fairy Queen. Right now, a hearty round of applause for Cicely as she receives her Coronation cup, saucer, teaplate, knife, fork and spoon set!"

I suppose, upon reflection, it took all of fifteen, maybe twenty seconds for the result to impress itself upon Father's brain. The polite, if half-hearted applause was just tailing off, when he exploded.

"Ow the bloody 'ell can you judge 'er the winner?" he bellowed, pacing forward. "What the 'ell's a soddin' Fairy Queen got to do wi' British 'istory?"

Cicely now stood clutching her award and trembling as her Mother placed a comforting arm about her shoulder.

"The decision is solely Mrs Aspinwall's and is in no way negotiable," replied Mr Willett trying to sound authoritative, but unable to conceal a waver in the voice.

"'Tis only 'cos she's a bloody varmer's daughter. She ought t' be disqualified!"

"I assure you," replied Mr Willett, nervously looking around for support, "that social status doesn't come into it!"

"Ah, you pull t'other bugger!" retorted Father, who by now had been joined by a small knot of similarly disgruntled parents, "The rules clearly stated all entrants must 'ave a British 'istorical theme!"

"Well, fairies are historical and British!" smiled Mr Willett, desperately trying to pour a little oil.

"Bollocks!" barked Father, employing a certain lightness of touch in his reply. "They don't even live in the soddin' village. They packs 'er off t' one o' these 'ere posh private schools, an' she turns up 'ere in a bloody party frock an' a yard an' 'alf o' tinsel and marches off wi' the bloody prize!"

"He's dead right, the rules clearly state all entrants must represent an aspect of British History," chipped in one of Father's new found allies, whose son, contentedly picking his nose, lurked some ten yards behind him dressed very authentically as Al Capone.

"Ah, you'm right!" agreed Father, "'Tis another prime example o' bloody Tories stickin' together t' tread down the workin' man. Guttersnipes all of 'em!"

For all the intimidating pressure Mr Willett would not budge. His expression was now that of a lame hedgehog confronted by a speeding 'Transit' van but, mustering every last ounce of fortitude, he bleated,

"The decision stands, and that's an end to it!"

"Right!" threatened Father, "We'll see you at the next village 'all meetin', I'm buggered if we won't!" Muttering darkly, he and his little band withdrew nurturing a deep sense of injustice. Almost immediately all the little historical figures, and one triumphant 'Fairy Queen' scurried off to the school cloakroom to change back into mufti.

It continued as a day of mixed family fortunes. Caggy and I displayed a total lack of co-ordination in the junior three-legged race, eventually finishing well down the field. The junior obstacle race degenerated into farce as I became hopelessly disorientated beneath the tarpaulin. Mother failed to impress in the parents' egg and spoon race, and was very much an also ran in the 'carry-a-piglet-in-the-pinny' dash. Father, on the other hand, was enjoying markedly more success. A disappointing fourth in the parents' obstacle race, he went on to shine brightly in the 'straw bale pitching', finishing runner-up. To cap it all he'd got a 'spare' in the 'skittling for the pig' and, with a score of fourteen, presently held the lead.

I was quietly minding my own business, watching Billy Lucas dispose of a string of challengers at the 'Jousting Lake'. Billy was one of a family of diddicoys that had abandoned their travelling ways just after the war, and now occupied a ramshackle cottage at the top of Folly Lane. He had held the position of school bully, and very successfully too, but he'd now moved on to senior school, much to everyone's delight.

The rules of the joust were that the winner stayed on until dislodged. As each new challenger was quickly despatched, Billy looked capable of claiming squatters' rights. I was just musing on how big and dirty and mean Billy Lucas looked when a familiar voice rang out behind me, and the blood in my veins turned to ice water. "My boy'll 'ave a go!" hollered Father, attracting the attention of Bill Walsh, Caggy's Dad, who was running the attraction.

"I don't think so Dad!" I squeaked, shooting another quick glance at Billy Lucas' brooding face.

"Rubbish!" said Father, and, handing over 2d. hoisted me onto the pole. "Grip wi' yer knees an' lock yer ankles" he advised.

Bill handed me my weapon, a saturated striped pillow. I looked along the pole to Billy. God, he was bigger than I'd thought, and his face was that of a ravening wolf contemplating elevenses. I locked my ankles, gripped fiercely with my knees, and braced myself to deliver the first blow. Out of the corner of my left eye, I noticed a striped pillow, which wasn't the one I was holding, heading towards my temple with gathering speed.

"You alright son?" queried Bill Walsh as he dragged me from the water.

"Course 'es alright! interjected Father "Wasn't ready was 'e!"

"I was Dad!" I quickly assured him.

"No you bloody well wasn't, t'other little bugger got the drop on yer! My boy wants another go!"

"No, no I don't, that's alright!" I gibbered.

"Tripe!" said Father, "Get up there!"

"That'll be another tuppence then!" said Bill holding out an anticipatory hand.

"Tuppence, be buggered!" replied Father, "That was no go, 'e wasn't ready!"

"I was, really I was! I don't have to have another go!" I offered hopefully.

"Shaddup!" he bawled, "and concentrate this time!"

"Alright!" said Bill conceding," My boy'll show un this time!" Father assured a couple of onlookers. "E's ready for 'n now!"

Of course he was right. There's no use in enduring experiences if you don't learn from them, and I'd certainly picked up a few pointers from the first encounter. I knew exactly what to expect this time. I locked my ankles, gripped fiercely with my knees, but instead of bracing myself, I relaxed and stared him coolly in the face, defying him to make the first move. Out of the corner of my left eye, I noticed a striped pillow, which wasn't the one I was holding, heading towards my temple with gathering speed.

"You alright son?" queried Bill Walsh as he dragged me from the water.

"What a bloody waste of tuppence you are!" sneered Father. "Go and find yer Mother an' get dried off!"

The culmination of the day was the inter-village tug-o-war. Father had gathered his team round him and was deeply into a pep talk. Everyone listened intently. Everyone that is except Roly, who was lolled back on the grass, seeing how far he could stretch the piece of chewing gum clenched between his teeth. Roly was looking slightly the worse for wear, with a large grubby plaster stuck over his left eyebrow. This was as the result of a drunken stupor he'd fallen into the previous Saturday, culminating in him walking into the back of the butcher's van. It looked as though the Heywood team were going to need all the pep they could get. I don't know what they fed them on over in Hawkridge, but my goodness they were some big lads. A fact not lost on Father,

"Don't worry about the size of 'em! he reassured his dispirited team. "Just remember, they 'aven't 'ad the benefits o' my experienced coachin', an' the bigger they be the 'arder they valls!"

The two lines of dreadnoughts faced each other.

"Pick up the rope," instructed the plummy-voiced umpire. The Heywood team flicked it up into their hands very professionally with the outside of their insteps. All except Roly who, smitten with a bout of nerves, had knotted himself into some enormous sheep shank, in attempting to secure his vast bulk into the anchorman position.

"Are you ready?" crowed the umpire, "Take the strain!"

The rope went taut as sixteen bodies plied their weight into it. Three equi-spaced ribbons, tied at its centre, trembled vibrantly.

"Pull!" he yelled, dropping his arm theatrically.

"Heave!" was the first and last thing Father shouted. For at that moment the three ribbons shot towards the Hawkridge team with the speed of a scalded cat, closely followed by eight bodies. The Heywood team were lying on the turf, a forlorn tangle of arms and legs, looking for all the world like a hastily discarded pack of spillikins. Hauling themselves dejectedly to their feet, they lined up for the change of ends. As the two teams crossed over, Father brandished an admonishing index finger at the Hawkridge lads.

"The slippery end that was. We'll 'ave you buggers in the next two!" he taunted.

The preliminaries were re-enacted, and upon the command "Pull!" Father's change of tactics became evident. "Hold!" he yelled, "Hold the buggers!" For fully half a minute both eights held. Not an inch was yielded. Muscles stood sculpted on straining thighs, knuckles whitened and rivulets of sweat trickled down over agonised grimaces. Suddenly, and without warning, someone at the back of the Heywood line lost his footing, and Roly came through them with the force of a runaway hogshead of cider on a one-in-three hill.

It was a total debacle. Father took defeat with customary ill-humour, offering only a scowl and the most perfunctory of handshakes to the victors. His day was completed when he ambled moodily over to the 'Skittling for the pig' only to discover that one of the Hawkridge lads had topped him with a score of sixteen. I thought he summed the whole day up pretty succinctly as we walked from the field. Aiming a full-blooded kick at an inoffensive bale of straw, he snarled "Bugger the soddin' Car'nation!"

A few weeks later it was the school summer holidays, and I was whisked off to Chichester to spend three weeks of unremitting purgatory with Gran.

Gran lived with her husband in a tiny terraced house whose garden abutted the ancient city walls. The husband, when spoken of, was never referred to as Grandad, Gramps or with any other of those customary endearments. This was due to the fact that Gran had married again late in life and, as far as I could judge at so tender an age, had very much drawn a matrimonial short straw. Always curtly referred to as Mr Williams, he held the position of family pariah, a role in which he seemed admirably cast. A dishevelled figure, with uncombed hair, a grizzled stubble about his chin, and clad in a rumpled, collarless shirt only half tucked into a pair of shabby brown bags, his life was spent spreadeagled on their threadbare ottoman, scratching himself and farting with a sulphurous venom. He seemed only to stir, reluctantly, for meals, and frequent trips up the garden path to the outside thunderbox, which was actually built onto the base of the old city wall. These functional sojourns seemed interminable, but eventually he would emerge, clutching a folded copy of the *Daily Herald* and, with braces still dangling about his thighs, his fly-buttons disengaged and a fag hanging from the corner of his mouth, he'd shuffle and hawk his way back down the path. Collapsing back onto the ottoman with a grunt, he'd invariably break wind again with a sonorous report. Whilst the crotch of his trousers was quietly smouldering he'd croak, "Another one for the King!" and smile quietly at his own tasteless drollery. As his favourite diet was faggots and peas, washed down with liberal libations of cream stout, the atmosphere in the house was rank in the extreme.

Gran, to her eternal credit, seemed to make light of all prevailing fetor, or perhaps her olfactory senses had simply been pummelled into submission. Whatever, she would sit contentedly in a high-backed windsor chair before her open range, absently humming a tuneless refrain, whilst the obscure garment she was knitting from multi-coloured remnants grew ever longer. She was a bony old crone, with ill-fitting dentures that shifted uneasily on shrunken gums. In the evenings, as the firelight cast grotesque, flickering shadows, and Mr Williams snored contentedly on the ottoman like a somnolent polecat, she would delight in harrowing my young mind with chilling tales of ghosts and ghouls, witches and warlocks and bogeymen that came to tea.

Resting her needles in her lap, and impaling a slice of bread on a wire toasting fork prior to its cremation before glowing coals, she would impart to me pearls of empirical wisdom for my instruction and betterment. She always attempted to do this allegorically, but was, unfortunately, wont to mix her metaphors, as her frail old brain lurched periodically out of orbit. Her most glaring example could well, at some later date, be adopted 'down under' by the 'Alice Springs Unmarried Mothers Support Group'. Leaning forward, her eyes narrowing, she would fix me with imperious gaze and say "Phillip" (for she always confused me with a cousin called Brian), "Philip," she would say, "There's many a slip twixt two in the bush."

Accustomed as I was to living in the heart of the country, it seemed strange to lie awake at nights and hear the traffic swishing past. Motor cars however were not the only things abroad in the night. Mr Williams' bladder was less than roadworthy and stressed to its limits by copious amounts of milk stout, often cried out to him in the small hours for urgent relief. Given this weakness and with the privy lurking at the far end of the garden, it seemed a matter of common sense to keep a chamber pot under the bed.

The reverberant snores would suddenly stop, to be replaced by a hacking, phlegmy cough. The ancient bedsprings twanged musically as he swung his feet to the floor. I could hear him muttering oaths, snuffling and grunting like a foraging badger in a dahlia bed, as he groped blindly in the darkness for the po'. The tintinabulation, as urine cascaded onto enamel, rang through the house. He'd invariably round off the performance by breaking wind with trumpet-like stridency before depositing the po', with a metallic chink, against the cast-iron bed post.

It was this habit of failing to place the pot securely under the bed that caused Gran endless consternation. For often as not, as the night wore on, the corner of the blanket became untucked and dangled gently in Mr Williams feculent little offering. It was to combat this that she cunningly devised the 'four-corner change' as she called it, whereby the blanket was rotated one side at a time so that all four corners received an equal chance of contamination, thus presumably ensuring that no one corner rotted more quickly than the other three.

Winkles are not everyone's cup of tea, and certainly not mine. But Gran and Mr Williams were fixated on them. Twice a week, come hell or high water, Gran would don her thick coat, haul on her wellies, knot her headscarf, and board the bus to West Wittering. Mr Williams never joined her. In fact, I never recall him leaving the house at all. But with his malodorous propensities this was probably just as well.

"C'mon! Gran would squawk up the stairs. "Get up, or you won't come winklin' with me!" I feigned sleep. "C'mon," she would repeat a short while later. "If you don't get up you won't go to West Wittering!"

"But I don't want to go to West Wittering!" I replied with some feeling.

"Well, if you don't get up you won't go!" she insisted.

"I know, that's why I'm not getting up!" I rejoined, digging my fingers defiantly into the mattress. Rather third degree bedsores than a day at West Wittering I thought.

"Well you won't go if you don't get a move on!" harried Gran, blissfully oblivious to my mounting incalcitrance. She knew she had manoeuvred me into 'Hobson's Choice'. It was either a day at West Wittering, or a day alone with Mr Williams and his orchestral rectum. Even with the bleak prospect of old 'thunderguts' braying 'Another one for the King!' *ad nauseam* staring me in the face, West Wittering wasn't an easy choice.

I'd been winkling with Gran on numerous occasions, and the format never varied. I watched dejectedly as the green bus receded into the distance, knowing it would be hours before its return. It had deposited us on the roadside, atop the sea wall. From here the splendours of West Wittering were laid out before us. To the landward side of the road lay an area of desolate, rush-strewn marsh which seemed to stretch at least to Aberdeen. To the seaward we had the sea wall covered in a thick green slime. From this extended a seemingly endless expanse of jetsam-strewn pebbles, covered in a thick green slime, the monotony of which was only broken at intervals by the interjection of gnarled wooden breakwaters, covered in a thick green slime.

I sat on a relatively slime-free section of breakwater, watching Gran grubbing enthusiastically underneath pebbles for her little spiral-shelled quarry, and reflected quietly upon the merits of West Wittering. With its total lack of seaside entertainments and unspoiled, if bleak countenance, it exuded all the olde worlde charm of an abusive tramp. I could not, for the life of me, understand why any free-thinking winkle would choose West Wittering as home.

It was high summer. On beaches all along the south coast squeals of delight could be heard as hedonistic trippers frollicked in the gentle surf. Pedaloes plied the deeper waters, and Timothy Whites' Suncream was applied by the bucketful. But not at West Wittering. The sea was steel grey, half a dozen immature herring gulls moped dejectedly, and the keen wind cutting in from Spithead seemed to possess an almost Arctic edge. Even at three-o'-clock on 'a July afternoon West Wittering seemed to be bathed in that indefinable quality that compels snow geese to prepare for the long flight south.

Eventually the bus returned and, as it sped towards us, I couldn't help studying Gran's face. It was white with cold, and her dewdrop bedizened nose was raw with the attentions of a soggy hanky. Was it all worth it for a few winkles, I thought. Then, as we boarded the bus, the chirpy conductor looked down at her bulging canvas bag and said "Good catch today m' dear!" Deep in her rheumy old eyes I detected a twinkle of triumph. Yes, to her, of course it was all worth it, and somehow I suddenly felt very contemptible for even doubting.

Once home, Gran set about boiling her catch for tea. I came to detest the smell, but not as much as I detested the spectacle of their consumption. Still sprawled on the ottoman, Mr Williams balanced the plate of winkles on his distended gut, partly obscuring his gaping flies. With a gaseous grunt, he flicked out the little protective black cap and delved deep inside the shell with his darning needle. Unwinding the hapless little mollusc from its lair, he dropped it onto an extended furry tongue, which ferried it into his unsavoury maw.

Now, Mr Williams' eating habits were very much in keeping with the rest of his demeanour. He possessed no dentures, but had retained a solitary decaying tooth in his upper jaw, just to the right of centre, which Mother had often referred to as his 'Picklechaser'. Consequently, he masticated his food with some difficulty, and winkles seemed to present him with more difficulty than most. Noisily slavering and gumming them into submission with exaggerated jaw movements, as sputum and juices trickled from the corners of his mouth, he often reminded me of a very large lizard chewing a wasp. Having cleared his plate, he'd wipe the salivated cocktail from his chin with the palm of his hand, and transfer it to his shirtfront. Producing gas from both ends he'd then sink back onto the ottoman, replete.

The three weeks dragged by, but eventually Mother arrived by train to reclaim me. It was to be more than two years before I saw Gran again, and this time under very different circumstances.

We had vacated our fine bailiff's house at Heywood, on account of Father overstepping the mark and ejecting a rather well-heeled Farms Systems Advisor – who had been specifically requested to call by Father's boss – from the farm premises, accusing him of being a 'snivelling Tory bloodsucker!'

We now occupied one of the more familiar types of tied cottage. Semi-detached, it was of brick and flint construction, with stout outer walls, a sound roof, and little else. The window frames were rotted and could not be opened. The inner walls were of a flimsy hardboard construction, and as one door was slammed shut, another, somewhere in the house, flew open. There was no cooker, no bathroom and the twin privy was at the far end of the garden. This garden was shared by our next-door neighbour – a rather elderly retired gentleman who lived alone – called Alf Blunt. There was very little garden directly to the rear of the cottages but it spread away some fair distance to the right and the various vegetable plots were divided by a veritable network of paths. These, if taken in the correct sequence, eventually led to the twin brick-built privy at the very extremity of the garden, nestling under a venerable Bramley tree. Its construction was interesting in as much as it had obviously been conceived originally as a two hole 'sociable'. A single elm plank spanned the width of the building, having two holes of the necessary dimensions bored in it. At a very much later date, someone had decorously erected a flimsy wooden partition up the middle, although the area beneath the plank remained undivided. Beneath each hole sat a sturdy oval bucket. Ours was removable through a wooden frontal hatch. Alf's hatch had long since disintergrated!

If both were occupied there was no privacy. Every deposit, every rustle of the paper, every wrinkle of the nose could be clearly heard. In fact, Father and Alf often had long and meaningful discussions sat over their respective buckets.

In the summer months these buckets hummed with a vengeance, and it seemed that every able-bodied fly in the southern counties had been drawn there – as the disabled to Lourdes. It could be most disconcerting, sitting there quietly pondering the universe, with a couple of wrothful blow-flies dog-fighting around your nether regions.

Old Alf's apparent answer to this was to light up his trusty briar. This smelt even more objectionable than the buckets, if that were at all possible. I don't know what he smoked in that thing. 'Reconstituted goats-droppings' Mother used to reckon, and Mother was seldom wrong in such matters. But whatever it was, it certainly kept the flies at arms length.

At this time, toilet rolls were things that other people used. The *Daily Mirror* was carefully torn into rectangles and impaled on a nail in the wall. Father took great delight in carefully tearing out the pictures of prominent Tory MPs and members of the Royal Family, and using them intact. A profound, if simplistic, political comment. It always fascinated me that when newspaper was exposed for long periods to the contents of the buckets it turned quite a vivid shade of pink. Periodically, Father emptied these contents into a pit dug in one of the vegetable plots, and just to be neighbourly he also opened the facility to old Alf. When suitably filled, the pit would be covered in with earth, and marrows planted on top.Some unsuspecting hospital matron was going to be presented with a whopper this Autumn, judging by the volume of this pit's contents. Father was well pleased by the prospect

A prospect which didn't please Father quite so much was that of having Gran to stay for a while. Mother had eventually pecked him into acquiescence, insisting that a peaceful stay in the country would help her overcome her recent bereavement. She had, a couple of weeks previously, discovered Mr Williams, with his trousers and a copy of the *Daily Herald* in a heap about his ankles, slumped on their outside toilet seat. It was perhaps fitting that he had expired on the thunderbox. The whole family naturally assumed that she'd be overcome with grief, but I thought she looked pretty chipper about the whole thing.

It wasn't Mr Williams' passing that was to cause her grief on her stay with us, but a misfortune that befell her on the second day. It was about 8.30 in the evening, and pitch dark outside, with intermittent scuds of rain borne on a mischievous March wind. I was perched on the draining board having my knees scrubbed when Gran toddled into the kitchen. Apparently, she was in dire need of a visit to the place beneath the venerable Bramley tree.

"The batteries 'ave gone in the torch Frank!" Mother hollered into the living room, "and Mother's got to go'"

"No bloody peace is there?" responded Father, who was trying to listen to a football commentary on the wireless, "Ain't there none in the sideboard? Top right 'and drawer'"

Mother rummaged negatively.

"Can't see any!" she replied.

"Bugger it, 'ave I got t' come an' do everythin'?" replied Father, beginning to sound aggrieved.

"It's alright!" Gran assured them. "I knows me way. I can find it without the torch'"

"You be careful!" Mother clucked, as Gran disappeared through the door still buttoning her raincoat.

Some moments later, with Mother still scrubbing furiously at my knees, there was a scratching and a sobbing at the back door. As Mother reached it, the door flew open, and there stood Gran, a woeful sight, covered from head to toe in reeking effluent and pieces of vivid pink newspaper. Unbeknown to us at the time, she had failed to negotiate the maze of paths correctly in the darkness. Taking a left instead of a right at the purple sprouting had been the fatal mistake which put her plumb on course for Father's cess-pit.

"Mother's fallen down your 'ole!" my Mother yelled through to Father.

"Well, for Christ's sake don't bring 'er in 'ere!" he blared, appearing in haste at the kitchen door. "Scrape 'er off, an' sluice some water down 'er out there!"

Father could always be relied upon to get his priorities right in a crisis. Mother did what she could with the water she'd been using to wash my knees, before scurrying around placing kettles and saucepans full of water on the range. Gran was distraught, and gibbering tearfully on about her aged frailness and pneumonia and her new raincoat, whilst Father resolutely stood guard.

"Don't worry about all that," he chided her, "thee's just make sure thee dussn't wander off thik coconut mat afor the bath's ready!"

I was still rooted firmly to the draining board, socks rolled down, and my knees wet. Father rounded on me, "Don't just sit there gawpin," he growled, "Shift yer arse and drag the bath in front o' the fire. Then bugger off t' bed. Yer Gran's got some sprucin' up t' do!"

Gran left three days later, and I was never to see her again. She died the following autumn. Perhaps, if God has a conscience, a shadowy, stooped figure can still be encountered on quiet and moonless nights diligently turning the pebbles of West Wittering's foreshore.

Probably the greatest irony was that her mishap was all so pointless. The marrows never were planted on their sumptuous bed of ambrosia. Father had a contretemps with his employer, refusing to work Sunday overtime at haymaking. True to all known form this escalated into a heated confrontation, with Father grabbing his employer's lapels, thrusting him against the cowshed wall and threatening,

"One more peep out o' you, and I'm buggered if I won't knock both yer eyes into one!"

Those were the chosen passwords which saw the milkmaid/airedale duo renew their acquaintanceship with the zinc bath. On the day of moving Father carried out one last act of rancorous vengeance, by depositing the contents of the privy bucket squarely on his employer's front doorstep.

6.
Pussums, Deckchairs
& Mercy Benders

WITH ITS ARMS wrapped around the sylvan perimeters of Longleat Estate, the sprawling parish of Corsley was to be the next brief stopover in our seemingly endless rustic peregrination.

The cottage was remarkably habitable, being acceptably weatherproof, within walking distance of village amenities, and boasting both inside toilet and bathroom. I sensed immediately that it was all too good to last; but I would bask in the rays of modern civilization whilst I could. The village could also boast a junior school of, apparently, very high repute. I benefitted from its tutorage for only three weeks before summer holidays intervened.

Six weeks of solid parental responsibility was always more than Mother could bear to contemplate. So the annual spectre of selecting some unfortunate to whom I could be farmed out for a fortnight or three weeks once again raised its ugly head. Father suggested his youngest brother, my Uncle Len. He had three children of his own. One more wouldn't prove over burdensome.

"We're not sending 'im there!" said Mother, adopting an offended expression. "Well, 'e sed 'e'd 'ave 'un!" replied Father. "An' that's good enough fer me!"

"That's not the point!" insisted Mother, hackles rising, "He maybe your brother, but he's nothing more than a womanizing trollop-hound. I'm not 'avin' 'im exposed to those kind of carryings-on at his age. He's not going there and that's an end to it!"

My youngest cousin Mark had just been whisked off to hospital with the mumps when I arrived at Uncle Len's the following Saturday. It had only been a twenty-minute journey in the Land Rover which Father had borrowed from the farm.

"I think 'es 'ad the mumps!" Father assured Aunt Enid, "Or were it the measles? Thee's know I can't rightly remember which 't'wer.

67

Still don't matter overmuch, I s'pose 'ers gotta catch the bugger somewhen er t'other, an' er?" So saying he slammed the Land Rover door with a metallic clatter and, pausing only to light a fag, was gone.

Cousins Maureen and Barry were both about my own age. Maureen one year older, and Barry eighteen months younger. They'd both had their bout of mumps some three years earlier. So, it eventually transpired, had I.

The three week stay was to prove eminently forgettable, except for one afternoon in a meadow behind their house. It was one of those idyllic English summer days, so often depicted in cereal and shampoo advertisements, but so seldom encountered in the real life. From a cloudless sky the sun patiently warmed capricious zephyrs. Borne aloft, scores of fluff-head dandelion seeds, fleeing their inveterate pastoral clocks, parascended gently back to earth. Birds carolled, bees droned, and lecherous gentleman grasshoppers abraded their inner thighs with an ever mounting stridency, wishful that some young lady grasshopper of compliant nubility might hasten to amorous dalliance amongst the Timothy grass.

I lay supine amid the buttercups, idly chewing the vinegary sap from a sorrel leaf. Fascinated as I watched darting swifts scythe the balmy air, I mused on how they could fly at such speed with scarce the beat of a wing.

"Ow about playin' cows?" twittered Maureen, who had approached stealthily and now stood over me silhoetted by the sun.

"Eh! What! Play what?" I jibbered, jolted from my reverie.

"Play cows," she repeated.

"How d'you play cows?" I queried, raising a hand to shield my eyes from the sun that was now forming an aura about her figure. I had no wish to appear ignorant but it was a game that had not hitherto fallen within my compass.

"'S easy!" she replied, "Look, I'll be the cow, you be the bull, and what can Barry be?"

"'Ow about a bullock?" I said hopefully.

"You mean one of those that's not really a cow or a bull?" she clarified, "Yea alright!"

I sat up and looked around. Barry was a short distance away. Having carefully peeled the bark from a hazel stick, he was now gainfully employed in stirring the end of it energetically around in a relatively fresh cow-pat. There was every indication that he lacked

*"Ow about playing cows?" twittered Maureen, now silhouetted by
the sun.*

the necessary enthusiasm to throw himself wholeheartedly into the
little farrago Maureen had planned. I was somewhat uneasy about
the role of bovine eunuch being foisted upon him. For, had he inheri-
ted even a small percentage of his Father's genes, then this was a
slipshod casting of the highest order. You see, Uncle Len had a local
reputation with the ladies. Known colloquially as the 'Ram of Bruton',
he was to marital fidelity what Attila the Hun had once been to the
Roman Commission for Fine Arts.

Whilst I pondered this point, Maureen was already down on all
fours, with her face at grass-top level.

"I'm grazing!" she said. "Aren't you going to be the bull?".

I must admit I was feeling a trifle self-conscious, but nobly launched myself into the part. Clenching my fists to my temples, and extending index fingers forwards, I proceeded to charge about and blare a bit. Pausing occasionally to snort and paw the ground with my foot, I looked every inch the scourge of Pamplona.

"Aren't you going to help me get some milk for milking time?" Maureen asked coyly, as I determinedly charged a singularly disinterested Barry from behind.

"'Ow do I do that?" I asked in all innocence.

Raising her flimsy summer skirt, and revealing a pair of regulation blue school bloomers, she said,

"You can stuff these full of grass to make an udder!"

Snatching up handfuls of lush grass I thrust them down the front of her capacious knickers. She carried on 'grazing', occasionally mooing solicitously. Eventually, I crammed her drawers to bursting point until buttercups and seed heads of meadow fescue protruded errantly from the elasticated legs. She continued 'grazing' awhile, her distended 'udder' suspended beneath her, before saying matter-of-factly,

"Right, it's milking time!"

"What me again?" I choked, "Don't the bullock do anything?"

I looked to Barry for help. He'd abandoned his hazel stick, and now sat with vacant expression decapitating dandelions between index finger and thumb.

"Don't just sit there playing 'Granny-pop-out-o'-beds!" I railed, "Come 'ere an' get the milkin' done," but my plea fell on deaf ears.

"Alright!" I said, wearily conceding defeat, "Just 'ow do I do the milkin'?"

"You just take all the grass out again!" she said airily, "So that my udder gets smaller again, just like a cow's does'"

As I groped around inside her underthings, vainly trying to locate the last few elusive strands of perennial rye-grass, I couldn't help feeling that there was more to producing milk than a bull stuffing handfuls of summer grass down the front of a cow's step-ins. Instinctively, I knew that there was something else, very fundemental, that bulls did to cows, but at that moment, for the very life of me, I just couldn't put my finger on it.

My innocence in such matters was to receive a severe mauling when, some weeks later, having returned to school, I was exposed suddenly to the seamier side of life. Terry Beesley it was who was responsible for catapulting me into the world of the sexually aware.

It was an early October morning, misty and dank. A small knot of boys huddled in the corner of the playground during the morning playtime, covetously admiring Stevie Denslow's brand new Dinky Daimler Ambulance, when, without warning, Terry dropped his bombshell. "I know the proper name for a woman's whotsits!" he sniffed, curtly removing a pendant dewdrop from his nose with the cuff of his jacket.

"A womans whotsits?" we all chorused.

"What, y' mean 'er titty things?" asked Freddie Hayward, trying to clarify.

"Yeah!" replied Terry with the smug and triumphant look of one who just happened to have the Koh-i-noor diamond in his lunchbox, and would, for a bite of your 'Wagon-Wheel', let you have a nifty peep.

"Cor, c'mon then!" we all brayed excitedly, "Spit it out, what is it!"

But suddenly, Terry, obviously realizing he held a very marketable commodity, became strangely reticent! We were just about to turn him upside down and physically shake the information out of him, when the whistle went for the end of the break. Everyone kept their eyes on Terry during class. Not that he could have gone anywhere with the priceless information, but it seemed the expedient thing to do.

"Right, books away, quietly now, dinner break!" instructed Miss Russell in her clarion Welsh voice. "Don't all rush!" she chided. But she was ignored. A self-appointed posse had already surrounded Terry before he'd got through the classroom door. Borne bodily, feet barely touching, he was deposited in the corner of the playground next to the dustbins – traditionally plotters corner. As the pressing throng menaced, Terry's eyes moved nervously from face to expectant face.

"Well c'mon then!" hissed Badger Wilcox, threateningly. Terry was certainly cornered, but still strangely reluctant to hand over his life's savings. He was threatened with a black eye, a broken arm and public disembowelment but still failed to deliver.

"An' we'll tell everyone about you and Lucy Herridge!" a voice intoned from the back. At last, we'd found his Achilles heel.

"Alright!" said Terry, licking his lips with the savoury anticipation of what they were about to utter.

"They're called Pussums!"

"Pussums?" we all repeated incredulously.

"Yeah, pussums, I 'eard my Dad say it last night!

Well that was it then. If Terry's Dad had said it that was good enough. He'd know about such things, after all said and done, he was a hospital janitor. So for the following fortnight 'pussums' reigned as the playground buzz-word.

The threat of exposing Terry's 'relationship' with Lucy Herridge was no empty one. For a couple of weeks after we'd returned from summer holiday it had been noticed, by the more eagle-eyed among us, that Terry and Lucy had been sloping off somewhere during dinner breaks. They were certainly very adept at it – at one moment they were there, the next they'd evaporated into thin air. No-one detected their going, nor knew where they went, but all save the most naive had deduced their purpose.

The truth came to light very strangely in class one afternoon. It was during geography, whilst Miss Russell was attempting to justify half the world's landmass being coloured pink, that a stifled chuckle from the back corner had her wheeling sharply round from her wall map and yelping.

"Beesley stand up! So the British Empire is amusing is it?" she continued with ill-concealed sarcasm. "Perhaps you'd like to tell the class in your own words, exactly which bits you find funniest!"

We all turned round, prepared to enjoy Terry's public execution. It was then, as Terry stood gaunt eyed and trembling at his desk, that the more observant amongst us discovered the truth about him and Lucy Herridge. For there, slowly emerging from his trouser-flies was a confused and succulent green caterpillar. So that was it. He and Lucy had been stealing through the gap in the hedge that led to Miss Russell's school house vegetable patch. Beesley had been having his wicked way with Lucy Herridge amongst the brassicas, and we now knew this. It was indeed a terrible power to hold over a fellow being.

In the few short weeks we'd been conducting our various bits of prepubescent research into the shadier side of ladies' naughty secrets, Father had not remained idle. He'd been cultivating an invaluable aquaintance up at the local pub.

Stan Reakes was in his seventies and had spent all his working life as a coppicer in the estate woods. He was immediately earmarked by Father as a useful contact for firewood and rabbiting. So it was, after many pints of ale, that Father and I paid him a visit one Sunday morning. He lived with his homely, taciturn wife in an isolated cottage with sparse, humble furnishings and an all pervading smell of wood smoke. He was, and always had been, it seemed, more that content with his lot. His earlier years had been primarily spent coppicing hazel and sweet chestnut for hurdle and spar making. As those crafts waned he turned to cutting out, as he called them, 'Pay 'ood', 'Banestooks' and 'Jumpery 'ood' or, to the layman – peasticks, beansticks, and jumpwood. The jumpwood was the twiggy branches of the silver birch cut and bundled in winter, and used to construct National Hunt steeplechase fences. He'd lived all his days enfolded by the woods and possessed a stoically gentle philosophy on life. He also retained a beautifully unspoiled dialect, one of the great features of which was his tendency to lapse into glaring malapropisms when attempting to tackle the names of any objects not familiar to his world. So it was on the day we visited.

"Me nephew works as a mechanic up to Rob Walker's garage," he informed us, as a beam of delight spread across his weathered features. "Thee's know, wur they've got all these voreign cars. Er took oi up thur yes'day addernoon fer a squinty. Caw, they got all these 'ere little Fidgets, an' Alfny Rominums and these 'ere bloody gurt Mercy Benders. But thur be one brand new little English car they got thur that they d'reckon be main wholesome, and they do call 'e a little Locust'"

A few weekends later we visited old Stan again to collect a load of logs Father had smooth-talked him into cutting. Having borrowed a tractor and trailer from Father's employer, we'd arranged to meet him at a predesignated spot in the woods. Stan had arranged for his wife to bring his lunch out to him, a walk of about a mile through the woods. About half way through loading we noticed him take a pocket watch several times from his weskit pocket and consult it agitatedly. Eventually, withdrawing to a nearby tree stump, he sat down, pushed his cap back off his forelock, took his watch out yet again, and studying it intently said, half to us, half to himself,

"Yer tiz na top zide t' quarter to, 'n 'er baint cum already. Bain't goin' ave oi on these 'ere strings an' ookum many more times sooner neeat lately. 'Unt come now, sure to. If 'er do us'll turn 'er back!"

I could happily have sat for hours listening to Old Stan's quaint and mellifluous tones, little realizing that in a few short years their like would delight the ear no more, but the first mechanical saw had been heard in the woods, and the first runner bean had twined its way up green plastic netting. Stan was a living dinosaur. Extinction for his kind was sadly imminent. Society may yet, given time, adjudge it a most terrible waste.

A few weeks later I was to become the victim of terrible waste myself. Perhaps, in retrospect, I may have been in a minority of one, but I considered my role in the School Nativity play as the criminal waste of a latent thespian talent.

I'd never been involved in a school production of any sort before, and when Miss Russell asked all those interested in taking part in the School Nativity to put their hands up, I swear mine was highest of all. I flushed with an inner pride as my name was added to the list.

"I'll deliberate over the weekend!" pronounced Miss Russell, completing her list, "and I'll tell you your parts on Monday. That will still give you plenty of time to sort out your costumes with your parents!"

I was awash. My mind raced in fantasy. Would I play Joseph with a slow, James Stewart drawl or with a touch of the Methods, leaning on the crib scratching meself? Or perhaps the role of one of the Three Wise Men might lend itself to the steel-eyed Albert Finney approach. Even the brief appearance of the Inn-Keeper would come alive with a spot of Kenneth Moore bonhomie. Ah, the possibilities were endless. Whichever part I landed, I felt an inner conviction that I would shine. I was restless to tread the boards.

The weekend dragged and saw me come into conflict with Father. Like all God-fearing men he had planned to spend Sunday morning sweeping the living room chimney. With all the furniture pushed back and covered in sheets, kneeling before the hearth he inserted the brush up the flue, agitating it vigorously before screwing on another rod. Swivelling on one knee he pointed towards the back door.

"Why don't you make yerself useful?" he asked "Get out in the back garden, an' gi' oi a yell when the brush do break out o' the chimmuck!"

I was halfway down the garden path, having almost mastered the pigeon-toed, stiff-legged, hip-swinging John Wayne gait, thinking it ideal for the entry of the Angel of our Lord, when Father's voice rasped out behind me,

"Thik brush come out yet?" he asked, glowering in the doorway.

"No!" I replied, casting a hasty affirming glance at the chimney pot.

"'S bloody funny!" he mumbled, half to himself, as he turned and shuffled back inside.

I was just getting the correct inflection in the thick Irish brogue of the 'lowly shepherd' when the voice boomed out again.

"I've only got one rod left, it must be out be now!"

"It's not – look!" I assured him pointing up at the chimney." Not that one you daft, half-baked sod!" he growled, "The one at t'other end!"

I nervously followed him round to the front of the house. The brush was out alright; so far in fact that its following rods had bowed under the weight and it now swayed airily outside the bedroom window.

"Buggered if it ain't a waste o' good food rearin' you!" Father observed, glaring at me darkly. "No bloody idea at all, yer as wet as a well-digger's arse!"

Monday morning saw the playground a-twitter with expectation. Everyone seemed convinced they'd land a plum part. Miss Russell made her eargerly awaited announcement after morning hymns. The classroom was bathed in total hush. She started by casting the Narrator, followed by Joseph and Mary, the the rest of the cast in descending order. When she'd announced the third shepherd and I still wasn't amongst the list of runners and riders, I began to feel a dark cloud of doom folding in on me. Still she plumbed her way to the depths of the list, before announcing,

"And the donkey at the manger – Toby Dyer!"

I was mortified and in consequence my performance, I knew, would be threadbare.

What was Miss Russell up to? The casting defied belief. The Narrator was fair enough I suppose. Melody Brice was academically brilliant. A scholastic high achiever if ever there was one. She could already, at the age of ten, do the eight times table without showing the working out in the margins. But how Lucy Herridge, after her dalliances amongst the purple sprouting, landed the part of the Virgin Mary I will never know.

Trevor Wolstenholme, the most proficient stutterer since Emperor Claudius, was being asked to hold down the part of Joseph. Whilst the three Wise Men – Badger Wilcox, Pip Duxbury and Kevin Smith – would spend rehearsals squabbling furiously over the single communal brain cell at their disposal. Brian Pascoe, the sturdy yeoman innkeeper, would habitually eat coloured chalks whenever he could lay his hands on them, and the Angel of the Lord was being portrayed by the inimitable Terry Beesley. His only qualification, as far as I could see, for playing the part was that he'd brought us all the glad tidings that the correct name for a woman's mammary appendages was 'pussums'.

As rehearsal followed rehearsal it gradually dawned upon me that I was the only one without a speaking part. Even Felicity Wise, as the oxen, was permitted a couple of doleful moos. I consoled myself that it was a lacklustre production anyway. A fact borne out by the employment of an ancient china-faced doll with a chipped nose and a tendency, when laid down, for one eye to close and the other to remain open, as the Infant Jesus.

The evening of the performance saw the school packed with babbling parents, or in my case parent. Mother had arrived to lend support, but Father had a darts match. The cast was milling around in the wings, in some very unconvincing costumes. Mine, in truth, was as unconvincing as anyone's. A pair of cardboard ears, cut from a cornflake packet, and wired under my chin. Lines were being gibbered repetitively. I stood and watched, unconvinced that any last minute rehearsal was going to polish my performance as a mute jackass with a crib fixation.

The stage had no curtain, it was just a case of trooping on and off from behind a screen. There was a straw-filled washing basket stage centre and, hung from a drape at the rear, an enormous tinfoil star. The lights at the rear of the classroom were extinguished. A blanket of hushed expectancy fell of the audience, and Melody Brice stepped jauntily into the spotlight.

"Emperor Caesar Augustus," she intoned, with a self-assurance far beyond her years, "had decreed that the world should be taxed. Each unto his own city. Joseph and Mary went forth from Nazereth in Galilee unto Bethlehem in Judea. The journey was long, and Mary, heavy with the child of the Holy Ghost, was tired and exhausted when she reached Bethlehem. Joseph bid her rest awhile as he enquired at an inn for a room for the night." Joseph – alias Trevor Wolstenholme in an ill-fitting black beard, staggered onto the stage, banging his broom handle staff far too theatrically on the boards. Clutching his arm was Lucy Herridge, looking about as virginal as Mae West in a latex peephole brassiere.

At this point I must confess that although not truly *au fait* with the concept of virgin birth, I did feel that the Holy Infant being swaddled and tinsel haloed in the basket of straw, stage centre, even before Mary and Joseph reached the hotel foyer, was stretching the bounds of credibility just a touch.

Trevor and Lucy did a U-turn at the far end and hammed their way back across stage. Pausing at the edge of the screen, they'd appeared from behind; Trevor rapped on it feebly with his knuckles. A tragically gormless figure in a striped tunic appeared in response. It was Brian – 'my goodness, is that what day it is?' – Pascoe, the humble innkeeper. At that very moment the steely fingers of stage fright closed vice-like around Trevor Wolstenholme's larynx. He dried, gulped audibly, licked his lips, then launched into an uncontrollable fusilade of stuttering:

"Is Eh' - is Eh' - th' - th" He paused, gathered himself, and took another run at it. "Is th' - is th' - th'-th'-th'.'"

Brian's head was by now hanging forward, nodding slightly in encouragement. His mouth dangled open and his lips silently mouthed Trevor's stammerings as he desperately tried to pick up the cue for his one and only line. At the third attempt, after an initial hiccup Trevor swept triumphantly through."Is th'-th' - is there any room at your inn?"

Brian, caught temporarily off balance, almost replied in the affirmative, changing the course of Christian history. But in the nick of time he hauled himself back from the brink, uttering the immortal line,

"No, but there is a stowly label!"

Halfway through 'Once in Royal David's City' the guiding star in the East somehow detatched itself from the drape at the rear of the stage and fell down behind my legs. I was suddenly aware of Miss Russell frantically gesticulating from the wings.

"Toby!" she hissed, "hang the star back up!"

A difficult one this, for turning to face the back of the stage presented a certain problem. Not one of showing disrespect to the makeshift Holy Infant with the Nelsonian squint, but much more prosaically being unable to turn my back on the audience owing to the word 'Kelloggs' being emblazoned across the back of my cardboard ears.

I did eventually manage, via a series of contortions, to relocate it, but some five minutes later it went walkabout again when its supporting sellotape gave way.

'We three Kings of Orient are!' heralded the entry of the three likely lads, each bearing a parcel. But once at the crib none of them could remember who had the Frankincense, who had the Myrrh, and who the communal brain cell. All the while, five simpering nymphets from the infants' class, dressed in the most perfunctory sheep's costumes, pranced and baa'd coquettishly stage front.

There were moments when I doubted whether the proverbial curtain would ever fall. Eventually however, to the clatter of hollow, nepotic parental applause, we all scampered off stage. All, that is, except the lazy-eyed 'Son of God' who, with tinsel halo now at a drunken angle, was abandoned to his festive fate. With the strains of 'Little town of Bethlehem' still ringing in my head, I tore off the pair of hated cardboard ears and, without remorse, crushed them into a waste paper basket.

The Christmas edition of the local Parish magazine contained an article on the play, fulsome in sycophantic praise. It made mention of most of the cast, singling out performances it considered to be of particular merit. Almost at the very end I at last received my due artistic critique 'The donkey,' it said, 'was played by Toby Dyer'.

My next run-in with a donkey occured during the following summer. I was sat astride one on the beach at Swanage. If its inscribed brow band was to be believed, it gloried in the name of Brandy. An ill-disposed little beast it was, with a jaundiced eye, a sullen, 'Roll-on-October' expression, and chronic, progressive tail mange. And there was little doubt it viewed my being on its back with great distaste. The rest of the group were some fifty yards distant along the tideline. Encouraged by a voluble, stubble jowled attendant, they were progressing at a crotch-jarring trot. But not my miserable steed. Steeped in a 'Bugger this for a seaside holiday' philosophy, he lay back his ears, dug in his toes, and steadfastly refused to budge. There was suddenly a sharp thwack behind me; Father had approached unseen and, obviously sensing I was not getting value for money, had brought a rolled-up newspaper sharply down upon the donkey's rump. In one cataclysmic moment the donkey failed to respond, totally. The colour rose in Father's neck.

"Shift yer scrawny arse, you idle little bugger!" he bawled, "Or I'll stick me boot up it six lace 'oles!"

Brandy responded by fixing him with a baleful glare, "I've encountered scores of day-tripping pillocks like you." he seemed to be saying. "and don't try the newspaper again. In my time I've run the full Fleet Street gamut, from tightly rolled *Daily Mirrors* to neatly folded copies of the *Financial Times!*"

Father, changing tack, grasped hold of the bridle and began to heave. The language grew steadily more profane, but at going nowhere, this donkey was unquestionably a seasoned professional. As a last resort, Father tried jabbing straight fingers into Brandy's short ribs, but he was not about to be moved. Realizing this, I slid quietly from his back. No sooner was the sand between my toes than he released a stentorious bray, and cantered at speed along the shore to reunite with his chums.

Father, changing tack, grasped hold of the bridle.

"Perhaps you' ll spend yer money on summat a bit more sensible now!" reproved Father as he stalked back up the beach.

We were enjoying, if that be the word, one of Father's darts team outings. There were usually two a year, and they were almost invariably to Swanage or Weymouth. Occasionally we also booked onto a coach operator's day excursion or the odd mystery tour. Regardless of how these trips were organised, I always found them a veritable cornucopia of embarrassment and looked forward to them with a pathological dread. It seems there always has to be a court jester on these trips, a barrack room organizer, a jovial, hail-fellow-well-met renderer of bawdy songs, and instigator of silly childish games. A self appointed lieutenant to the driver, who always knows a prettier route than the one being taken.

I was never sure exactly what elements in my Father's upbringing saw him so admirably qualified to fill all these roles, but he slipped into them with consumate ease. True, he did play the mouth organ, or 'gobbo' as he colloquially called it, to an acceptable standard, and he did possess a remarkably thick skin, but above all there lurked in his very psyche an unquenchable desire to be the life and soul of every gathering he was part of, even when others were virtually crawling under the seats to escape his attentions. The pub outings invariably saw the coach trundling along with so many crates of ale stacked in the boot that the front wheels seemed only periodically to touch the tarmac. Inside, the occupants, already feeling the effects of alchoholic libation, were being treated to a selection of Father's filthy songs.

"Thee's all know this 'un now!" he'd announce, playing first verse and chorus on his 'gobbo' before launching into 'Chase me Charlie', grab the leg o' me drawers!' or perhaps 'Susannah's a funnyful man!', complete with grunts, whistles, and sundry lavatorial noises. Then there was 'The Candlemaker's Daughter', a catchy, up tempo number, liberally spiced with phallic innuendo, plus numerous other tacky little ditties garnered over the years.

Egged on by the more bawdy and dissolute on board, and with confidence bolstered by alchoholic intake, Father's lyrics constantly plumbed new depths of bad taste. The less salacious amongst the passengers attempted to disassociate themselves by gazing fiercely out of the windows or squirming visibly in their seats. I tried joining these more genteel elements by staring intently at the passing countryside, attempting to disown him, but was eventually reduced to squirming and cringing. Mother, on the other hand, inured by years of constant exposure, sat through it all blank-faced and unheeding, whilst in her lap she clutched a brown paper bag full of tomatoes, her sovereign remedy for travel-sickness.

My embarrassment was always further heightened upon our approach to the resort. As, spotting the blue of the English Channel for the first time, Father would leap to his feet and excitedly exclaim,

"Look Toby, the sea." Then, addressing anyone who'd listen, would continue, "It's in 'is blood thee's know. 'Ers goin' t' be a sailor when 'es old enough, just like 'is Dad!"

By this time my discomposure had me shrivelling on my seat like a deflated balloon.

Father's ad hoc organization did not stop at offensive songs. He was quite capable of organising gambling games too; in fact he usually felt compelled to do so. One such was notable for creating a fracas on the seafront at Weymouth. The coach had just arrived and most of the passengers disembarked. Mother and I were, however, still on board putting an end to a brace of egg sandwiches.

There was suddenly uproar outside the coach somewhere near the rear. Eager to investigate, I scampered along the aisle and pressed my face to a rear window, just in time to see Father lifting all five feet three inches of Wally Compton bodily from the ground by his jacket lapels. Father had not held a soft spot for Wally, ever since being beaten by him in the area qualifying rounds of the *News of the World* Darts Championships.

Ever the one to bear a grudge, he had seized upon this opportunity to display his advantage of size and aggression over skill and artistry. The baying mob surrounding them seemed split about fifty/fifty between those who would pacify and those who would cheerfully toss Christians to lions. The altercation had apparently stemmed from a dispute over the result of a little wheeze Father had thought up called 'Wheelarch Roulette'. It was normally a harmless diversion, and simple enough in practice.

Before the coach departed Father chalked a 'pointline' on one of its rear wheel arches. Each passenger was invited, for a one shilling stake, to make an initialled chalk mark on the tyre-wall. The winner of the kitty being he whose chalkmark was nearest the 'pointline' when the coach came to rest at journey's end. On this occasion it appeared that Wally's mark, and that of Stan Latham, a renowned braggart and debauchee, who also knew most of the words to Father's songs, were equidistant from the 'pointline'. Not surprisingly, Father had adjudicated in favour of his crony. Wally had reacted with what, in retrospect, might be adjudged an ill-considered remark to the effect that with eyesight like that no wonder Father couldn't progress beyond the *News of the World* qualifying rounds. This, allied to his marked lack of physical stature was the reason Wally now dangled with his toes about two inches above the promenade.

As Father drew Wally to eye level and spat the words "Slackgutted little weasel!" in his face, our coachdriver saw fit to make a timely intervention. The show over, the mob dissolved, and I felt an overwhelming urge to roll up into a tight little ball and evaporate. Neither had I forgotten the Mystery Tour the previous summer when Father had pressed everyone on the coach to try and guess their destination, at half-a-crown a go. We ended up at Lyndhurst in the New Forest, and the coach driver gleefully pocketed 37/6d.

Father's presence on the beach was a none too edifying spectacle for an impressionable young son to adopt as a role model. Not for him the role of strutting bronzed Adonis, flexing sculpted pectorals, and blithely hoofing large quantities of sand up the nostrils of sundry cowering bantam-weight inadequates. He was more your quiet, low key beachmaster type. Draped in a hired deckchair with trousers modestly rolled half way up parchment-white shins, braces dangling in repose, and the daily paper veiling his face, he snored in somnolent oblivion. Disturbed occasionally by an over-inquisitive wasp, he would stir into semi-consciouness and swat at it half-heartedly, as a gasp of resignation expelled from deep within his lungs caused the edge of the newspaper to flutter fitfully. Once in a while he might rear up, like a malevolent bull walrus, roaring at some hapless child whose bouncing beachball had encroached too closely. This apart, he normally spent the day sprawled inert, waiting for the next lot of egg sandwiches to come up.

The sum total of his conversation for the day was usually "No!", spoken through the incumbent newspaper, in response to my requests for small change to spend on any one of a number of seaside entertainments.

There were occasions on which he stirred, and I was left dearly wishing he hadn't. I well remember that on one particular visit to Weymouth Father took an uncustomary interest in the Punch and Judy show. It was shortly after Randolph Turpin had successfully challenged Sugar Ray Robinson for the World Middleweight title. This fight had aroused public interest in general and Father's interest in particular. Exhibiting great enterprise, the Punch and Judy man had added an extra dimension to the end of the show by having two dusky boxing glove puppets representing Turpin and Robinson staging a return bout.

Father had heard about this, but I hadn't, and was puzzled by his sudden interest. We leant on the sturdy promenade railings, gazing down onto the Punch and Judy stall and the assembled heads of scores of enthralled youngsters squatting on the sand. Father seemed passably entertained by the traditional part of the show. I don't think he much appreciated the plot as such, but with babies roundly beaten with rolling pins, policemen being summarily executed, and the crocodile garrotted by a string of sausages, I think the violence quietly appealed to him. Eventually, Mr Punch, adopting the role of M.C., announced in his reedy, swozzled voice,

"The World Middle Weight title return; and in the blue corner from Leamington Spa, England, the reigning Champion, Randolph Turpin!" an announcement greeted by heady cheering from the audience. "And from the United States, the former Champion, Sugar Ray Robinson!" Apart from the rustle of sweet papers – silence. I had glanced at Father's lips during the announcement, they had silently mouthed every word. The two puppets moved centre stage, circling and weaving, then came together in a flurry of action, with little flat leather gloves slapping furiously.

By now Father had been sucked into the spirit of the contest as shoulders hunched, head bobbing from side to side in animated defence reflex, he moved clenched fists in short, hooking movements. Suddenly the Turpin puppet collapsed on its back after taking a flurry of slapping blows. Mr Punch took up the count, "Four – five – six".

"Get up y' silly bugger!" bellowed Father, his coarse, guttural voice incongruous above the pervading juvenile babble. At the count of Nine a hairtrigger wrist jerked Turpin upright again and hostilities were resumed. Father was still very animated as round one neared completion and Turpin rallied. I suddenly realized that the crowd had melted from around him and, in isolation, his antics began to look even more absurd. People were glancing one to another and sniggering quietly. I desperately wanted to slink away and shrivel.

Round two opened with a brief flurry that saw Sugar Ray laying prone. "E's got the bugger!" crowed Father, turning to me, his face a picture of delight. As the bout continued, a petite blonde girl aged about twelve moved amongst the audience on the sands, gently rattling a collection box. A short while later, her flaxen hair strewn by a capricious breeze, she climbed the steps to the promenade. Her progress had obviously not gone uncharted for, as she reached the top of the steps, Father grabbed me by the arm, and with one final glance at the two scrimmaging puppets, propelled me swiftly along the prom observing, "Thee's don't wanna bide an' watch thik infantile rubbish!

In general it would not be unfair to say that Father was not given to the enthusiastic pursuit of seaside pastimes. Rather than an active participator, he was more your informed observer, or at least until gently warmed by the sun and permeated by tepid stout, his mind curdled into somnolent oblivion. I'd never witnessed him kicking a beach ball or cussedly disputing a 'french cricket' decision. Neither had he ever demonstrated an overwhelming compulsion to let me bury him up to his neck in sand or to help with the digging of a trench to channel seawater into a sandcastle moat, although I do recall one instance when, whilst my back was turned scouring the foreshore for a flat lollipop stick which I would press into service as a drawbridge, he derived enormous satisfaction from demolishing the east battlements of a particularly handsome castle I'd taken ages to build, by lobbing an empty stout bottle with unerring accuracy from the sanctuary of his deckchair.

Simple, God-given pleasures, like feeding the gulls, called upon far too many mental resources and kindly humane instincts. In a fit of pique, however, he did once hurl one of Mother's fairy cakes at a particularly raucous individual that had ventured too close. The misguided creature swooped upon it, wrestled with it, attacked it voraciously with its bill, made not one whit of an impression and, giving second best, retired, crest-fallen, to a nearby breakwater. However, of all seaside activities, I sensed that Father nursed a particular loathing of water sports.

"No natural buoyancy, that's your trouble!" he diagnosed, almostspitting the words in contempt as I vainly attempted to master the rudiments of the breast stroke in about nine inches of water. Having been browbeaten by Mother into teaching me to swim, Father was proving a very disinclined coach indeed. There was little likelihood of him demonstrating the technique, as he was pattering around in ankle deep water, trousers rolled to just below the knee, 'box Brownie' slung from the left shoulder, still decorously wearing his trilby hat, and keeping a weather eye open for the four-inch wavelet that just might overwhelm him. My knees and elbows were fouling the bottom as I vainly went through the motions.

"Perhaps if I tried it out a bit deeper it'd be better!" I suggested.

"No, dussn't wanna get out o' thees depth!" said Father sternly, obviously envisaging wet trouser bottoms if he were called upon to assist me.

I persevered for a while, but made no progress. Meanwhile, Father's attention had drifted to two comely young things frolicking in the water nearby. An errant ball splashed down a few feet from him. Moving more quickly than I'd hitherto seen him in seaside surroundings, he plucked it from the water and, with pronounced affectation, lobbed it back towards them. It was followed by some licentious remark with which he showed signs of being obviously well pleased. But, caught on the breeze, it was carried away landward and solicited no response whatsoever from the two beauties at whom it was aimed.

By this time, fast running out of ambition, I was stood upright in the water."Ah, given up then!" Father observed, scarcely able to conceal his delight. "Don't understand you, buggered if I do. Zwimmin' ought t' be in yer blood. Natural I wuz, zwim like a bloody vish. When we wuz in the Med, off Crete, us use t' 'ave t' dive overboard an' zwim twice around the ship afore us wuz allowed back on board fer brekvust! I'd be out t' thik headland an' back now if I 'ad me costume."

Trailing back up the beach we were confronted by Mother.

"'Ow did it go?" she enquired cheerfully.

"Oh, best part of a waste o' time," replied Father. "Never got off the soddin' bottom. Not an ounce of natural buoyancy in the little bugger, can't fathom it. Not a bit like 'is Father. Thees' knows me, born t' water I wuz, zwim all day and dive like a bloody Kingfisher!"

On an ensuing trip we tried the swimming bit again, but with distinct shades of *deja-vu*. Indeed the nearest I ever saw Father come to exhibiting his much heralded prowess at 'swimming like a fish' and 'diving like a Kingfisher' was when, having stepped backwards into a water-filled sand hole at Swanage, he hopped unsteadily on one leg, cursing vehemently, and wringing sea water from his trouser bottom.

Strangely, although the overbearing life and soul of any coach journey, once at the beach Father usually sought isolation from the others on board. This didn't normally prove too difficult, as they were usually going to great lengths to ensure that there were at least half a dozen breakwaters between themselves and him. So it was perhaps a little surprising that on this particular pub outing to Weymouth we should find ourselves amidst a little knot of fellow trippers.

Someone had suggested going as a group to one of the little cafes in town for a fish 'n' chip dinner, and Father was proving a bit dilatory about the whole thing. Reluctant as he was to forego the traditional fare of gritty egg sandwiches, tomatoes and Mother's seagull-proof fairy cakes, he was even more apprehensive of having to pay for his deckchair upon his return.

"Well, if you've fallen on such hard times, Frank, I'm sure we can organise a bit of a whip round for you when we get back, if they charge you again," said Barney Cresswell with just the hint of a wry grin. Now this was proof positive, if indeed proof were needed, that

Father was feeling a trifle off colour, for normally a playful little badinage of this nature, particularly emanating from Barney Cresswell, of all people, would have been as a red rag to a bull. We all held our breath for the customarily rancorous pedestrian riposte, but it failed to materialize. Suprisingly so, because Barney had long stuck, like a jagged pebble, in Father's craw.

A tall, gangling man, with kindly, yet academic features and large humorous blue eyes, Barney spoke softly yet with clipped precision, in almost cultured tones. His quiet self assurance and extensive vocabulary marked him out as something educationally poles apart from the rest of the hoi-polloi down at the pub. Yet he seemed to delight in their company. Always willing to embrace their monosyllabic repartee, Anglo-Saxon profanities and stunted witticisms with a kind, avuncular understanding and tolerance. He often dropped pearls of wisdom into otherwise barren public bar conversations, and could seldom be cornered in an argument or proven wrong.

Father had a love of occupying centre stage over a pint with his cronies, and consequently viewed Barney's apparent popularity with considerable distaste. At every given opportunity he would attempt to get one over on him, but was normally dumped squarely on his metaphorical backside by Barney's superior learning and quicksilver mastery of the English language. For all this, there were no lofty pretentions in Barney. He was the most easy-going and affable of men. Spending his days tending a less than thriving market garden, his clothing was as rundown as his business, and his sole delight seemed to be quaffing ale in the Blue Boar and imbuing its patrons with a little homely wisdom and worldly knowledge. Because he chose never to speak of it, no-one really knew of his background. Rumour and speculation were apparently rife in the pub at one time that he had been a Battle of Britain hero; one of Churchills famous 'few'. But as it transpired the claims were just a little over optimistic. There were three perfectly sound reasons why Barney's exploits had never set the skies ablaze over Kent. Firstly – he'd never had the good fortune to be posted to Biggin Hill. Secondly – Barney had never actually flown a Spitfire in anger, and, thirdly – he had spent the war as a lance-corporal storeman in the Somerset Light Infantry.

Even Father was forced to acknowledge that the café we'd chosen had provided an excellent fish 'n' chip dinner.

"Nothing like a bloody good blow out!" he gasped, loosening his belt a notch and unfastening the top two fly buttons. He belched sonorously, suddenly remembered where he was, and apologised without an ounce of sincerity. We all arose from our tables feeling suitably replete.

"Shan't be able t' zwim 's addernoon on a vull stummuck!" announced Father in a manner which suggested a couple of trips around the bay employing a medley of strokes would be a pretty normal after-lunch enterprise.

We'd walked but a few yards down the street from the cafe when the Gods suddenly smiled upon Father. His golden opportunity to get one over on Barney Cresswell was offered to him gift wrapped. Parked at the kerb on the opposite side of the street was a huge, powder blue American car. Typical of its era, it was all chrome, fins and whitewalled tyres, looking for all the world like some hideously overstretched juke box. "Just look at that will you!" exclaimed Barney, "Isn't it just so awfully tasteless. Typical American ostentation!"

Father scoffed audibly. Having thus momentarily attracted the attention of the group, he theatrically cast a sideways glance at Barney, then, adopting an expression of the utmost disdain, lifted his eyebrows to the heavens. He stepped out into the road and marched purposefully across, stopping in front of the shimmering monster. He stooped slightly and peered intently at the leading edge of the bonnet. Then, as if to confirm what he saw, smoothed his fingers slowly across it. As he straightened up a smile of triumph cracked his face. In that moment you sensed, from his very demeanour, that at long last Father had got one over on Barney Cresswell, and was about to savour it fully.

"Well!" he shouted back across the road, "there's a bloody know-all for ya'! It's not an Austin at all, it's a soddin' Buick!"

Father retreated under his newspaper for the afternoon and became dangerously quiet. There was little doubt he was bruised by his howling and very public blunder; also by the injustice of having to pay again for his deckchair as he'd mislaid the ticket.

His spirits rallied somewhat a bit later on when his comrade in mediocrity, Stan Latham, turned up bearing a bottle of brown ale. At 6.30 pm we all made our way back to the coach, parked on the promenade nearby the Jubilee clock, and clambered on board. I'd just returned to my seat, having been ordered by Father to jettison a slimy length of bladder-wrack I was hoping to take home for meteorological purposes, when he pounced again,

"Thee's still got any sand in thy shoes?" Receiving an answer in the affirmative, he continued, "Well thee's get out t' the edge o' the prom and empty 'um down over. Thee's can get theeself arrested fer stealin' sand from the beach. S'pose everybody were to take 'ome a shoeful o' sand, there'd be bugger all beach left!"

As I returned, empty shoed, Father was outside making his way to the rear of the coach. The driver had started her up and was just letting her tick over gently. As I climbed in yet again, I couldn't help noticing that Father had by now reached the middle of the road, and was holding up in his hand like a constable on point duty. Reaching my seat, I peered out of the window to see him still holding up one hand, palm outwards, whilst, with the other, he was obviously beckoning our coach driver to reverse. The coach moved not an inch, but quietly burbled away on idle. By now there was a line of at least half a dozen vehicles on either side of Father, who still retained basically the same pose, save that his beckoning had now become noticably more animated. Still the coach did not budge.

It was the time of evening when everyone, having enjoyed their day, was on the move and keen to get home, and by now two lines of stationary vehicles tailed back for some considerable distance – and one or two drivers had located their horn buttons! Father was, by now, gesticulating wildly and, with face beginning to twist with rage, he was mouthing something I could not quite hear, and by the look in his eye and set of his jaw I was thoroughly glad I couldn't. At this point, with the cacophony of car horns building, the coach-driver calmly turned to Barney Cresswell, who was sitting opposite him occupying the 'door' seat, and said with weary resignation,

"Go and tell that silly old sod to come in will you. We're waiting for another three to turn up yet."

I looked for a deep, dark hole to accommodate me. There wasn't one.

The journey home followed a time honoured pattern. We'd scarcely cleared the outskirts of Weymouth before Father, producing his 'gobbo' from an inside pocket and standing up in the aisle, one hand hanging grimly onto the overhead luggage rack, launched into taste-less vaudeville. A particularly vulgar recitation encompassing nuns, vegetable marrows and crisp frosty mornings opened his account; to be followed by a startlingly virtuoso performance of 'Sweet Peggy O'Neil.' True, some of his lyrics – 'She might charge a tanner, She might charge a bob,' and – 'Sweet Personality, Takes on matelots for charity,' might not have been immediately identified by the more avid

Music Hall afficionado, but Father was going down a treat with the bulk of the inebriates on board. However, a couple of limericks that would have made a Tyneside stevedore blanch solicited a rebuke from the driver,

"Oi mush!" he hollered back over his shoulder, "Tone it down a bit will you. There's women and kids on board remember!"

Father was unabashed, and, pausing only to top up on fluids, he threw himself into the next racy rendition; and like a real trooper he carried on until sweat dripped from his brow. As we headed into Frome he rounded off his act with a touchingly sentimental little number entitled 'John's Brown's donkey had a pimple on its nose!'.

With a final flourish, he tucked away his 'gobbo' and, picking up his cap proceeded to do what he always felt compelled to do at the end of every journey. He toured the coach making a collection for the driver. The collection completed he chasséd unsteadily down the aisle. Upon reaching the front he placed his right hand on the chromed guard rail to the rear of the driver in order to steady himself and, with cap balanced carefully in his left hand, leaned forward to display the spoils. It was at this very moment an oncoming motorist decided to contest the gap between two parked cars. In an instant the driver locked solid, pistoning both feet into the floorboards. His arms were rigid, knuckles blanched and tiny bloody vessels stood out in relief on his temples.

The coach slewed to a shuddering halt and we were treated to a classic demonstration of cause and effect. As it rapidly decelerated, Father accelerated with equal rapidity, and was catapulted headlong into the footwell. Coins of the realm flew into the air and showered down upon the shaken driver, most of them ending up somewhere beneath his foot pedals. Making a less than understanding gesture at the motorist, who had adroitly side-stepped catastrophe, he turned grim-faced towards Father who was still hauling himself to his feet. Once upright, he straightened his jacket, then checked his 'gobbo' for signs of damage. The driver slowly shook his head in a mixture of anger and despair.

"You planning on coming on many more of my bloody outings?" he asked sardonically. Father declined to answer, but he certainly was.

A lesson learned from life invariably stuck with Father, but not always to his advantage, as was graphically illustrated a year or so later, on one particular trip to Swanage.

The morning spent on the beach had followed the well-trodden furrow. Hired deckchair, rolled up trousers, dangling braces, boiled egg sandwiches; in fact all the trappings of unbridled hedonism were on display. At lunchtime, without disturbing the daily paper covering his face, Father idly stretched out an arm towards Mother. Palm open, he agitatedly crooked his fingers a couple of times to communicate his impatience. Responding as a hen reed warbler might respond to the gaping bill of a surrogate cuckoo fledgling, Mother dutifully deposited an egg sandwich into the twitching hand. Father was just ferrying the sandwich under the edge of the newspaper when a sudden, unexpected gust of wind playfully whipped the covering from his face and sent it sailing, piecemeal, down the beach.

"What the buggery!" yelled Father, clambering from the recumbency of his deckchair, in the hope of retrieving his paper. But he was much too late for by now it was nearing the tideline, its component parts spreading ever wider as it went. "Sod it!" he barked, clenching his teeth in fury. Then, in a fit of childish petulance, he theatrically dashed his egg sandwich to the sand. "Well I'm buggered if I'm shelling out fer another paper!" he snarled, rounding on Mother, as though she'd just suggested that he should.

"Silly," Mother mildly scolded, "very silly, that was the last egg sandwich. All there is left now is four slices of my treacle cake!" At the sound of those words my heart sank. I saw Father wince slightly and visibly recoil. Mother's treacle cake was indeed a strange and forbidding phenomenon.

The recipe, we believe, was once given to her at the door by a dishevelled and vindictive old gipsy crone from whom she had declined to purchase lucky white heather. As a curse, it was fiendishly subtle, yet insidiously chronic. The resultant glutinous mass came to command a sort of deference not even accorded to her other numerous culinary fiascos. It wasn't for eating. It was treated more like a small pet terrier – taken on day trips, but always safely borne home again. If four pieces were brought out then assuredly all four pieces returned. Mother never responded to this but, as with her 'plaster of paris' fairy cakes, she habitually carried on churning them out. Eventually they'd end up being thrown out for the birds where they'd lie with even the most resourceful of sparrows giving them a wide berth, until eventually eroded by wind and rain. I was strangely reminded of Mother's treacle cakes many years later when Harrier jets were flying on sorties during the Falklands conflict and

Brian Hanrahan 'counted them all out, and counted them all back'.

A small boy scampered up clutching part of Father's newspaper. Looking suitably pleased with himself he announced,

"This is yours innit mister? I caught it blowing down the beach!"

"What good's a couple o' bloody pages?" snapped Father. "Go on, bugger off!" The startled lad needed no second bidding before spinning on his heels and making off across the beach like a long-dog.

"Caw! look see at that!" Father exclaimed, gazing out across the bay in the general direction of Old Harry Rocks. "It's as black as yer 'at over Bournemouth! I bet they're 'avin' a right basinful over there!" he smirked, rubbing his hands with glee.

There was nothing quite like other people's misfortunes for lifting my Father's spirits. But, had he cared to look behind him at that moment, he would have appreciated that other people's misfortunes were about to become his own. For looming over the Purbecks there came a great, glowering purple bruise of cloud. He'd hardly got the words 'Damn good job that's skirtin' round us!' out of his mouth, before the first few harbinger droplets pitted the sand. In response the beach began to clear quite rapidly.

"Best get over the road to them shelters in the gardens!" said Mother scrabbling our effects together in haste.

"That's alright!" replied Father. "Thee's do what thee's want, 'tis nuthin' more than a scud, 'twill be over in vive minutes! I baint about to leave these 'ere deckchair an' pay for'n again. I got too well caught at Weymouth last year if thee's remember!" So saying, he collapsed the deckchair, grabbed his gaberdine raincoat and trilby from Mother, and announced,

"I'm goin' t'set the chair back tight under the prom wall an' cover meself wi' me mac. 'Tis comin' from thik way so most of it will pass I over!"

It was obvious that quite a few people had also been caught out by over-zealous deckchair attendants in the past. For, as Mother and I left the beach, I noticed they too had adopted Father's plan and were nestling hard under the promenade wall covering themselves with rain coats.

By the time we'd reached the concrete shelter the rain had picked up a bit and was now a pretty steady downpour. We joined the huddle of fellow trippers inside who were moaning and complaining as only seasoned British holidaymakers can. Suddenly, and without warning, the steady downpour gave way and the very heavens opened.

It was now a good old-fashioned cloudburst.

For ten minutes we watched as the deluge continued, and the wet gravel path outside turned at first into a stream and then into a rushing brown torrent. I had totally dismissed Father from my mind, absorbed as I was by the spectacle, until Mother mused,

"I'm not sure your Father was very wise!"

The bedraggled figure that appeared in the doorway a few moments1 later seemed to bear out her observation.

"Buggering 'ell!" bellowed Father, managing as usual to capture the quintessential charm of the English language in one simple phrase, "What a bloody stupid place to go an' stick a storm drain, right behind where I 'ad me deckchair!"

From what we could make out, Father, in his haste to get under cover, had failed to notice the storm drain outlet in the promenade wall. The pipe had obviously been blocked with leaves and rubbish, as, for some minutes after the downpour had reached its peak, not a drop of water had seeped from it. A build-up of water must have suddenly shifted the blockage and it came out of the pipe like a cork from a bottle. The full force, catching the back of Father's deckchair, sent it, and him, careering many yards down the beach.

The rest of the day went badly. The coach driver could not be found to let Father back on board to dry off. He eventually sloped off to a gents' toilet where he partially succeeded in doing the job.

The brooding black cloud, flushed with success, surged out across Poole Bay, heading for the Isle of Wight where it no doubt hoped to surprise a few more unfortunates cowering beneath promenade walls. The sun returned to bathe the beach in warmth, and the air was very quickly filled once more with the clamour of children's voices, but Father's mood remained foul, even by his own taxing standards. His saturated trousers hung to dry on the back of the deckchair, as he sat with a towel spread across his lap, glowering,

"I don't see why I got t' 'ang about fer 'ours, soakin' wet, waitin' 'til every other buggers ready to go 'ome!" he complained. "I've 'ad enough o' soddin' coach trips. I'm goin' to get meself a car, then I can sod off 'ome when I feels like it!".

His words, spoken in pique, were destined to prove prophetic. It was to be the last coach trip ever taken to the coast in my boyhood.

7.
Double Standards, Rabbit Pies, and Nobbly Nutsticks

"JUST THEE'S TAKE A WANDER out an' 'ave a squinty at this!" beckoned Father, appearing at the kitchen door, his face incapable of concealing an unbridled self-satisfaction. As bid, Mother and I followed; out of the back door, around the side of the cottage, down the path, and out into the lane.

"Wha's think o' he then?" he beamed, "Didn't I just tell 'ee I'd get one?"

True, he had been threatening for some weeks to get a car, and true, he had arrived home with something vaguely resembling one. But no shining modern charger this, with sleek, rounded fifties styling, sitting taut on its chassis, exuding open-road virility and rarin' to go with boundless silken-geared *joie-de-vivre*. This was a venerable square-rigger, sagging wearily about its limp springs in broken-winded geriatric repose. Its shabby black cellulose had, over the years, been polished through in patches to reveal the red-oxide undercoat. Its chrome was pitted and lacklustre, and the spokes of its wire wheels looked dangerously rusted. Quite frankly it looked sickly and debilitated, and there seemed little doubt that, had it been a horse, trembling fingers would even now be extending towards the lightly oiled humane-killer.

"Goes like a rat up a pipe!" boasted Father. "'Tis a 1934 Standard Nine. That's when they wuz really buildin' cars!"

Mother looked moved to make a comment but, wisely one suspects, stifled the temptation.

By now I had made my way around to the front passenger door. I was just about to open it and hop in to see if those torn and sagging seats were really as uncomfortable as they looked, when Father edged a couple of paces forwards and bellowed,

"Don't thee open thik door, 't 'ave got a main dickey top 'inge.

Nuthin' I can't fix mind thee, but leave of un alone fer now!"

Peering in through the passenger window I could appreciate that the 'period' seating was complemented by holed and threadbare carpeting and peeling, water-stained veneer on the dashboard. In the passenger footwell there lay a sun-browned rectangle of once white cardboard, bearing the faded legend 'SOUND RUNNER. SNIP. £65.'

The following Saturday morning might, Father thought, present an ideal opportunity to take us for a spin in the new acquisition. The destination was to be the tiny town of Mere, where we'd do the weekly shopping. I had already clambered into the back when Father instructed Mother, who was heading for the front passenger seat.

"Thees 'll 'ave t' climb in over from the driver's side. Don't wanna bide an' caddle about wi' thik passenger door. 'Tis alright propped on the way 'tis, 'cos the catch be 'oldin' it in place, but fer Christ's sake dusn't thee open un, or as sure as eggs, thik top 'inge 'll give way!"

With the three of us eventually ensconced and full of expectancy, Father turned the key and pulled the starter. Much to my surprise, the engine instantly spluttered into life. I must admit I felt a small ripple of disappointment, as the vision of Father swinging wildly on the starting handle, thunder clouds gathering about his brow and vitriol pouring from his lips, had quietly appealled to me. But no, all credit to the venerable old girl. As Father released the clutch, she pulled smoothly away. Conveniently choosing to ignore the pall of blue smoke that trailed us down the lane, Father lapsed into a positive orgy of self-congratulation.

"Listen t' that," he warbled, "she's purrin' like a bloody pussycat. I tell thee, when it comes t' cars there's no bugger up t' pullin' the wool over my eyes! They gotta get up well afor sunrise t' catch Frank!"

Without mishap we trundled into Mere, and Father pulled up next to the kerb outside the Post Office. Mother, keen to be about her shopping, opened the door to get out. There followed a brief, but tortured rending of metal as the top hinge disengaged and its bottom partner gave way under stress. The door crashed violently to the pavement. As is so often the case, when you don't need one – there he is. Standing some twenty yards away, the constable, alerted by the metallic crash, turned, and with hands still clasped behind his back, sauntered ponderously towards us.

"You bloody stupid mare!" raged Father, his face rapidly becoming apoplectic, "I told you, didn't I, you soddin' cloth-eared imbecile, don't touch the bloody door. Now look, we've got the perishin' law bearin' down on us!"

Mother sat quivering and ashen. Father's withering tirade subsided rapidly as the constable approached, and with practiced ease he slid effortlessly into obsequious mode. Standing a foot or so from it, polished black toecaps glinting in the pale April sunlight, hands still clasped firmly behind his back, and rocking gently to and fro on the balls of his feet, the constable peered down at the offending door. With an expression of stone he addressed Father, who had, by now, clambered from the car and was hovering nervously in the region of the nearside front wing.

"Yours is it Sir?" Father nodded sheepishly. "Brought it with you did you Sir? Y'know Sir," the Constable continued in sardonic vein, "Rather reminds me of when I was a lad. My old Dad took me to see Bertram Mills Circus, and very good it was too. So, what are we to expect next then eh? All four wheels falling off Sir? Jets of steam shooting from the radiator perhaps? Or an enormous explosion and coloured smoke coming from the exhaust? You've got the makings of a show stopping act here Sir!" he continued, his face remaining totally impassive. "But I'm not wholly sure that Mere High Street is the place to present it!"

Father's face had taken on a hunted look. His eyes darted nervously, and he was obviously uncertain which way this was all going.

"Everythin' were alright 'til me wife opened the door, officer. Y'know what women are?" he fawned hopefully.

"I do indeed Sir," replied the Constable, "I've got one at 'ome meself. Not that I would expect her to do the car maintenance of course. So I would humbly suggest Sir, that you fix this back onto your vehicle in some way, drive carefully 'ome and get it repaired properly before venturing out again onto the Queen's Highway!"

So saying he turned to Mother, tipped the peak of his helmet, bid her 'Good morning' and, with ambling gait, was off down the pavement.

"Bloody old fool!" said Father quietly, before disappearing into a nearby greengrocer's shop and re-emerging with a length of twine. Beckoning me, he snorted, "Right, lets get this bugger tied back on before old smart-ass returns!"

With the door securely bound by coils of twine, and Mother instructed to clutch hold of the inside handle, we motored quietly out of Mere. "This bugger's goin' back these addernoon," Father announced on the journey home. "They can give I me money back, or summat more up together t' replace it!"

Sure enough, that Saturday tea-time saw him arrive home with something, he at least considered 'more up together'. The colour of the verbal exchanges that had taken place at the garage to secure the deal can only be imagined, but it had ended up costing him a further fifteen pounds.

Upon initial inspection it looked ominously like its predecessor. The same dated, rectangular outline, shabby cellulose and dazzle-free chrome. It too bore that cowed, round-shouldered look of the work-worn peasant labourer whose pitiful life had been wasted away in menial toil and forelock tugging servitude.

"Tis a Standard Ten!" announced Father vauntingly, as though going up a digit had considerably advanced him socially. "An' 'tis a year newer than t'other one!"

I was forced to admit that, apart from a section of the headlining that was falling down near the back window, the interior at least looked more presentable. It also had an operational front passenger door – a distinct plus! Whatever its considered merits, it only remained with us for just over a month.

One morning at breakfast, as Mother toiled at the sink, chipping lumps of burnt fried bread out of the frying pan, Father was lamenting his trip home from a darts match the previous evening.

"Bloody car!" he moaned, through part masticated egg and bacon. "Wouldn't pull yer soddin' 'at off! Right down in second I was. Then it only just spuddled over the top o' Blackdogs 'ill. Gutless it is, flat as a witch's tit. Goin' t' 'ave t' trade 'n fer summat else'!

'Summat else' did arrive home a couple of weekends later.

"A wasp, did you say, a wasp?" Mother bleated, querying Father's pronouncement on his latest dip into the used car market.

"Aye!, a bloody Wasp. A Wolseley Wasp!" rasped Father, his normally tissue-thin patience shredding before our eyes.

"Looks just like the other two t' me!" observed Mother, making a perfunctory tour of inspection.

"Like the other two! Like the other bloody two!" he repeated, his voice hopping up half an octave, and throwing in a well chosen expletive to add dramatic effect. "Listen woman, a 'undred an' ten pound this bugger cost me, an' taint no ordinary car. 'Tis a Wolseley I tell thee. They d' call it the workin' mans Rolls-Royce!"

"Isn't that the Rover?" I interjected foolishly." Shaddup, y' know-all little fart!" he snarled, rounding on me, his face a vengeful mask. "An' stop buggerin' about wi' thik indicator arm!"

"But it's not meant to be stickin' out like this all the time is it?" I asked.

"An' what the 'ell d' you know about it?" he bristled. "'Twill go down alright when I gets in, never you mind!"

"Well I reckons you've bought another load of trouble!" mumbled Mother, dolefully shaking her head and nervously wringing the hem of her pinny. Father, sensed the spawning of a conspiracy, and suddenly became defensive,

"Alright. Look, if you two buggers don't wanna ride in it, say so. 'Tis alright fer me t' work all the hours God sends, and t'make sacrifices t' get it, ai'nt it? Then all you can see fit t' do is pick 'oles in it!" By now his voice had taken on a wounded quality. "I'm tellin' y' Wolseleys is a different kettle-o'fish t' Standards. They'm precision built. The workin' mans –" He stopped suddenly, remembering he'd already made that claim and been shot down on it. "Anyhow," he continued, "they've even got a little 'luminated badge on the radiator that lights up at night so other Wolseley owners'll recognise thee even in the dark. An' you watch one o' these 'ere AA blokes, proper snappy salute they always do fer a Wolseley!"

Time was to prove Father's judgement of Wolseleys far superior to that of either Mother or myself. It was to prove a thoroughly reliable and trustworthy old family retainer, giving four years of ungrudging service.

As Father's confidence in its ability grew, he became ever more adventurous behind the wheel, and weekend trips took us gradually further afield. He remembered some obscure cousin he'd not seen since the first successful field trials of the wheel, and one Sunday morning we set off for Blue Anchor, a tiny village on the North Somerset coast, a few miles from Minehead.

Various enquiries in the village were met by a sullen lack of cooperation. Surly countenances appeared round partially opened doors. An eerie feeling of suspicion hung over the village street. But, with persistence, we eventually tracked down the whereabouts of Father's long lost relative.

"'Twill be a surprise fer the bugger an' no mistake!" chortled Father as we headed towards an address on the outskirts of the village.

Whether or not they recognised Father as we climbed the steep pathway to their bungalow, or whether one of the churlish villagers had telephoned ahead we never knew, but repeated knocking, ringing on the doorbell, and hallooing through the mock-Victorian letterbox solicited no response from within. Which was strange, for as we climbed the path I was sure I'd seen a shadowy form flit past one of the windows.

As we turned to leave, a young lad appeared pushing a heavy delivery bike, containing a small box of groceries and a Sunday newspaper laboriously up the path.

"Lookin' for Mr Cudlip?" he puffed, pausing for a moment, obviously thankful for a breather.

"Yeah!" replied Father, "can't seem t' make no bugger 'ear tho"!

"Oh they'll be in alright!" the lad assured him brightly. "Always are," he continued, "'Cos I always collects their money on a Sunday mornin'!"

With that the lad led us round to the rear of the bungalow. Leaning his bike against a small wooden shed he approached the back door. As he hollered, "Mrs Cudlip, its Peter!", he flung open the back door to reveal three adults cowering in the kitchen.

"There's someone here to see you!" he informed cheerily.

"Uh yes, yes, its uh, um, Frank isn't it!" stammered one of the two male fugitives "I, um, its er, well, I suppose uh, you'd better come in then!"

"Couldn't make no bugger 'ear at the front door. Bell not workin'?" Father railed, blithely oblivious to the atmosphere of discomfort that reigned.

The younger male, obviously the son of the house, suddenly remembering a pressing engagement, excused himself, grabbed his jacket, and fleeing past the non-plussed errand boy, disappeared without a backward glance.

"Uh, you um, remember Maud of course!" the older male said uneasily.

"'Course I remembers Maud!" replied Father a trifle effusively, "Thee's seems t' forget I knew 'er afor thees did. When she got caught out wi' thik matelot in the waitin' room down at Templecombe Junct—" Father was cut short as an armour-piercing elbow caught him squarely beneath the third rib, and Mother scowled darkly. "Oh ah!" said Father, regathering himself, "An' this is Gwen, an' my boy Toby." Then to us. "An' this is George, an' o' course, Maud!"

Anyone with a moderately sharp knife could at that moment have cut the atmosphere into blocks.

We were hurriedly ushered through towards an incredibly sumptuous lounge. Glancing back as we negotiated the kitchen doorway, I swear I caught a glimpse of Maud's gnarled fingers clamped in steely grip about the errand boy's windpipe.

"I expect you'd like a cup of tea now you're here!" said George icily. "Aye, 't would go down a treat," replied Father, thick skin still proving impervious.

The rattle of china and the stifled murmur of conversation emanated from the kitchen. Various snippets were just audible to the cocked ear. Father's name was mentioned, along with 'not the decent crockery' and 'ham fisted'.

The afternoon was spent in stilted conversation and boiled over reminiscences. I idled away my time visualising Maud's reputation being compromised by the rough familiarity of some uncouth naval stoker, on a wooden bench, amid the chocolate and cream livery of a dimly lit GWR waiting room. Judging by the physical evidence before me, it would have had to have been very dimly lit indeed. They seemed rather eager that we should leave before teatime, but Father failed to grasp this, and it was left to Mother to quietly impress upon him that we just might be in some danger of overstaying our welcome.

We left, with Father cheerily assuring them that now we'd found them we'd be sure to look them up again; and George and Maud, through gritted teeth, hissing "Yes anytime," – but not before we've moved.

Unbeknown to us old Dame Fortune, in vindictive mood that day, was to deal us another low card on the journey home. Leaving Blue Anchor we pootled quietly along the little coast road to the picturesque old village of Watchet. We parked nearby its tiny harbour, and whilst out stretching his legs, Father succeeded in upsetting a couple of beefy seamen, standing on the deck of a small timber freighter, by waxing lyrical about his days in the navy.

"Proper seamanship that were. Steamin' into all these 'ere voriegn ports, showin' the flag, gettin' all the local dagoes down on the jetty cheerin' their bloody 'eads off. Don't s'pose you lads gets a lot o' that just 'aulin' trees about!" As he concluded, he seemed oblivious to the fact that he was only moments away from considerable physical harm mounting the harbour steps towards him.

Having been fed with no more than tea and a couple of fancy cakes at George and Maud's, advanced peckishness was now setting in on all fronts.

"I'll pop an' ask them blokes on the boat if they knows of a decent pub where we can get a bite!" Father announced brightly. Mother, who was perhaps the more receptive to brooding airs of menace, wisely councilled against it.

"Why don't we," she hastily suggested, "try that village we turned off at on the main road. We passed a couple o' nice lookin' pubs there!"

So it was that we trundled into Williton and sat in the car impatiently awaiting opening time. When it came, Mother and Father disappeared inside at a controlled trot, leaving me still sitting in the car. Twenty minutes later, and smelling distinctly beery, Father reappeared clutching two bags of crisps and a glass of lemonade.

"Won't be long!" he said reassuringly.

Nearly two hours had elapsed and darkness was falling when they both returned. Despite the two bags of crisps I was still feeling ravenous and, if I wasn't sorely mistaken, they smelt strongly of something cooked.

"Only a couple o' pasties an' some chips!" Father replied, when I enquired. "You wouldn't o' liked 'em!"

"They don't normally do food on Sundays," interjected Mother, "but the landlady was ever so good, she could see we were 'ungry."

"Aye!" said Father "an' it stuck t' the ribs a treat an' all!"

Hoping to press for a least one more bag of crisps I said,

"I've still got the lemonade glass here!"

"I knows," replied Father, "'ow's reckon we got all t'others at 'ome?" and stirring the old Wolseley into life, guffawed delightedly at his own unleavened wit. As we headed homeward along the A39, twilight became darkness and a gentle drizzle became steady rain. We were threading our way through the small shoe-making town of Street, my mind still wrestling with the vision of two golden-brown, hump-backed pasties nestling amid a veritable field of chips, when suddenly another vehicle, lights glaring blindingly off the wet tarmac, bore down on us in what seemed to be the middle of the road. Father, temporarily dazzled, reacted by swinging the wheel vigorously to the left, hoping to avoid contact. That contact he did avoid, but there still came a thump, a violent jarring, and the rending of tortured metal as he shunted into another vehicle parked at the kerbside.

"You've 'it a Jeep!" squawked Mother.

"Jeep be buggered!" growled Father, peering through the rivulets of rain cascading down the passenger window. 'Tis a bloody Land

Rover. 'Course they be all this 'ere alloy rubbish, no guts to it, 'twill be a right bloody mess I'low. Lucky we'm in a Wolseley, all 'eavy gauge steel this, weighs well over the ton thee's knows. 'Twon't be that much 'arm done I reckons!"

So saying, he opened his door to get out. At the same instant the front door of the house behind the Land Rover opened, and two figures became silhouetted against the light as they tore out onto the pavement. For some ten minutes a heated discussion flowed. Then, suddenly, the back door next to me was wrenched open and Father's furious, bedraggled face appeared,

"Move yer soddin' arse over!" he snapped, "an' make room for this!" This peremptory command was followed in short order by the appearance of a severely mangled front wing, obviously torn from its moorings, that was unceremoniously thrust into the back seat next to me. Father's initial reading of likely accident damage had, it seems, failed to take into account the sturdy steel cross member that forms an integral part of the Land Rover's rear end.

Father, now a thoroughly rain sodden and dejected figure, clambered back into the car whilst both Mother and I, fearing the worst, tried to look as unobtrusive and 'not present' as possible. Then, to our complete bewilderment and lack of comprehension, having seemingly spent all his fury Father suddenly, and out of all known character, became quietly philisophical.

"Well!" he said, "could 'ave bin worse, an' old Reg out t' Hunts Garage 'll soon 'ave that straightened out an' welded back on. A quick dab o' Valspar an' Bob's yer uncle. Mustn't look too much on the dimpsey side o' things," he continued, wiping the condensation from the inside of the windscreen with the sleeve of his jacket. "At least we've brightened up old George an' Maud's day 'aven't we?"

True to Father's forecast the damaged wing was hastily repaired and given a hurried brush coat of paint. Gone forever were its former smoothly flowing contours. Its surface, now wrinkled and corrugated, rather resembled the carapace of a malnourished terrapin.

Unabashed by his contretemps with the Land Rover, Father still grabbed his opportunities at weekends to motor far and wide. Sometimes with a definite destination in view, sometimes just meandering through quiet country lanes hoping to stumble across a convivial pub around the next corner. The New Forest was the intended destination the day one of my earliest observations on the Wolseley came home to roost.

The summer traffic was heavy, and queues of vehicles had built up as we negotiated the narrow streets of Wimborne Minster. At a cross-roads in the town centre a police constable was on point duty, manfully trying to ease the log-jam of irate motorists. He was an imposing man, probably in his late forties, with an ample girth, minimum neck and maximum jowl. It was hot – very hot – and the constable, although in shirt sleeves, was obviously sweltering as he swung his arms in well practiced routine. His face was florid beneath his helmet, and dark patches could be seen on the material of his shirt about the armpits. Every once in a while one of his hands would deviate briefly from rehearsed routine as he quickly flicked off a dewdrop of sweat that had trickled to the tip of his nose.

He was coping well, but it seemed pretty obvious that the combination of heat, pressure and exertion were slowly taking their toll. His face was showing distinct signs of ill-temper. We approached, and Father, planning on turning left, activated the nearside indicator arm, which sprang out horizontally. Eventually we reached the front of the queue to be met by a baleful glare from the irate constable. He agitatedly beckoned Father to where he was standing. Father edged forward, and leaned his face out of the window.

"By Harry!" he toadied, "It's warm today!"

"Ideal weather for flying I s'pose Sir!" parried the constable sarcastically. Father gawped non-plussed, "Shall I clear the roadway so you can effect a take-off Sir?" he sibilated.

"Uh!" replied Father, by now totally bewildered.

"In short!" exploded the constable, "Which bloody way do you intend going?"

What none of us had realized up to that point was that, having taken a right turn earlier, the off-side indicator had failed to cancel and so we had approached the already exasperated police constable with both indicator arms sticking out like the wings of a taxying aircraft.

"Left t' Ringwood!" Father gulped lamely.

"Well!" growled the officer, knocking the offending off-side indicator down with all the force he could muster. "Put the bugger on this side away then!"

Mooching around quiet country lanes could be just as exacting for Father, as was graphically illustrated one Sunday evening in high summer. We were bowling along, minding our own business, going nowhere in particular, at a singularly pedestrian pace, all the time unwittingly heading towards a double-edged blow at Father's pride. The sunroof was open and, as leafy canopies passed intermittently overhead, I lay back in the rear seat and let the rush of balmy air wash over my face. My idle woolgathering was terminated abruptly by the piercing blast of a car horn. From the back window I could see that our sluggish progress along a lane too narrow to accommodate a passing manoeuvre was causing some irritation to a suave young buck at the wheel of a smart duo-toned Ford Zodiac. Time and again he edged out, hoping to find the lane widening so that he could overtake, but time and again the verge forced him back.

"Let the bugger wait!" said Father, "nobody needs t'be in thik sort o' 'urry on a Sunday evenin'".

For what seemed like miles we kept him trapped behind. Banging the top of the steering wheel with the heel of his hand, gradually gave way to animated gesticulations, as both the driver and his young male companion mouthed at us to let them by. But frenetic light flashing and horn blowing seemed to be making no inroads at all on the dog in Father's manger.

"Always were, an' always will be, more 'aste less speed!" said Father, philosophically.

Eventually we came to a T-junction and, as Father halted, the Zodiac cut past on the outside with two wheels mounting the grass verge.

"Get that bloody pram off the road you addle-brained old sod!" the passenger yelled from his open window. Then, engine revving furiously, the Zodiac careered off up the road.

"I'll swing fer them buggers if I catch 'em!" bawled Father, his neck suffusing with colour.

With steadily gathering speed, the staid old Wolseley, lurching through blind corners and rattling unforgivingly over numerous potholes, set off in vain pursuit. The chase lasted all of half a mile before, suddenly descending at speed down a sharp little hill, we ploughed spectacularly through a fast flowing ford. Water shot up in jets through the front footwells, soaking the legs of both Mother and Father. The former was still squawking in alarm as, about fifty yards beyond the ford, the engine coughed, spluttered and eventually died.

Muttering oaths Father climbed out, lifted one half of the folding bonnet and inspected the engine.

"Bugger an' damnation!" he cursed, straightening up and fetching the windscreen a vicious swipe with his cloth cap. "Bloody saturated it is. Goin' t''ave t' wait fer thik lot t' dry out, could be ages!" he moaned, consulting his watch. "Cor, pubs is open too. God I'm dyin' fer a pint!"

In the event it took about twenty-five minutes before the old girl stuttered back into life.

"Us best 'ead fer North Cadbury!" decreed Father, "there be a pub there wi' a 'alf decent cellar, an I'm as dry as a vish!" It seemed that his vendetta with the two dashing young blades had been temporarily expunged from his mind. But I knew that Father had an uncommon capacity for storing and nurturing rancour somewhere deep in his bile duct until such time as it was triggered to erupt and spew forth in vengeful malevolence upon anyone unfortunate en-ough to incur his displeasure. His thoughts, it seemed, were focused more upon the amber pint awaiting him than on the road ahead, for as we approached an oblique and unlined T-junction Father's speed lessened not one jot.

The strident blare of a car horn and the squeal of tyres were the first indications we had that the Singer Gazelle now bearing down on our starboard quarter was there at all. Father, assuming right of way, had bowled blithely on at the junction. The Gazelle driver, assuming likewise, had done the same. Slewing violently, the Gazelle driver took evasive action, eventually coming to rest hard against the offside verge. At the same time, Father, sinking his foot to the boards, brought the game old Wolseley to a shuddering halt.

As he scrambled out and stormed back up the lane, one could see steam visibly jetting from his nostrils. He was not in benevolent mood. His jaw was set in an aggressive mien, and the eyes were flashing hellfire and brimstone. His colour was up, and his dander had arrived at speed to keep it company.

"Bloody idiot!" he roared, "I'll knock both 'is eyes drew th' back of 'is thick skull!"

"For 'eavens sake calm down Frank!" Mother squeaked.

But her trembling little plea was lost on Father, and I must admit, in all honesty, if events were about to take their usual course, I'd rather hoped it would be. Street theatre was imminent. Father, reaching the Gazelle, stumbled through the rank growth of cow parsley overrunning the verge. Still cursing vehemently he reached the driver's door just as the occupant opened it.

"You stupid, thick witted tripe-'ound!" he raged, "What th' 'ell d'you think you're at. Got a wife an' kid in there!" he continued, jabbing his finger back towards us. "Could've bin killed, tearin' round like a bloody maniac!"

The Gazelle driver began emerging from his opened door.

"If you can't 'andle the soddin' thing, bide at 'ome an' do yer knittin'!" Father went on almost dancing with fury.

I had to admit it was going very well so far.

The Gazelle driver continued to unfold himself from the car, and it was fast becoming obvious that here was no timid and weedy little Sunday motorist. In fact, as his lower limbs began to straighten, Father's head gradually tilted back as his eyes attempted to follow those of his adversary. It then moved slightly from side to side as it took in the width of the shoulders. As this six-feet-nine-inch leviathan gradually uncoiled itself, the more accommodating became Father's tone.

"It's brainless buggers like you that causes the accidents!" quickly tempered to, "There were no way I were goin' t' see thee comin'! Mind you some o' these bloody lanes 'round 'ere be a death trap!" then to "Disgraceful I calls it, 'avin' no give way lines on a junction like this, plain askin' fer trouble. 'Twould 'ave given you right of way I suppose!" Then eventually to "I 'opes yer missus is none too shaken up. No 'arm done I 'opes. Sorry if I were a bit off 'anded there fer a minute, pretty shook up meself thee's knows!"

The Gazelle driver remained silent and impassive, apparently content to let his gargantuan physique do the talking for him.

"So if everythin's alright then!" fawned Father to the third button of the Gazelle driver's jacket; then, smiling weakly to acknowledge the female passenger, and backing slowly off the verge, he turned and strode back to the Wolseley. Slamming the door and casting a hasty glance over his right shoulder to confirm that the motoring colossus hadn't followed him, he grunted,

"That put the bugger straight. No good pussy footin' aroun' with these bloody idiots!"

There was one pub Father didn't swan around the country lanes hoping to find. He invariably made a bee-line straight for it. This was the New Inn at Shepton Montague. Since becoming part of the motoring fraternity he had adopted this rather bland village hostelry, some eight miles distant, as his 'local'.

As many as five times a week he'd wend his way through the back lanes. Having become so entrenched in its journey, one could well see the old Wolseley in the light of the aged, forbearing carthorse, plodding its way gently home between the waggon shafts, its handler snoozing blissfully atop the load of hay. It would have come as no great surprise had it turned up late one evening having made its own way home with Father sleeping off a skinful on the back seat. Almost without exception Saturday evenings saw us at the New Inn. I was left outside clutching crisps and lemonade whilst Father and Mother enjoyed the conviviality inside. I say enjoyed – in Mother's case I could perhaps be accused of hyperbole; borne with stoicism may well be closer to the mark. In the company of one or two other women of similar circumstances she sat on the bench to one side of the public bar. A half pint of Cream Label stout in a stemmed glass on the table before her, she clutched her handbag to her lap and stared absently into the fuggy atmosphere.

Father, on the other hand, was embracing the alcoholic bonhomie and tomfoolery of his small, but vociferous, band of cronies, foremost amongst whom was Joby Westcott, an arch buffoon if ever there was one. An amputee who had lost his right arm, almost to the shoulder, in a quarrying accident in his youth, he compensated for this with a larger than life personality and alcoholic capacity. Ribald in the extreme once drink had cast its spell, he and Father would vie with each other to see who could be the most outrageous, and still stay on the premises.

His favourite jape, and one repeated *ad nauseum*, was to sidle up behind some unsuspecting young filly at the bar, and drape the empty sleeve of his jacket over her shoulder, allowing the cuff to dangle about her cleavage. As she shrieked and recoiled in disgust, he'd holler,

"Don't worry m'dear, there's no 'arm in that!" and then proceed to fall about the bar, his one surviving hand clutching his lower ribs as they quaked with mirth.

Saturday evenings always seemed to follow the same format, and by nine o'clock Father and Joby would be 'entertaining' the rest of the pub with a seemingly inexhaustible repertoire of filthy songs. More often than not Father had, by this time, clambered onto one of the bar tables, and with one foot tapping out a rhythm in a shallow pool of beer slops he'd artlessly render such melody as there was on his 'gobbo'. Manipulating the mouth organ with only the thumb and forefinger of his left hand, left his remaining three fingers free to clutch the rim of a metal beer tray on which the right hand drummed out a rhythmic tattoo. Joby, despite only having one arm, was an absolute wizard on the spoons and often occupied another bar table as his performing podium. The two of them became progressively more inebriated as the evening wore on until, reeling with intoxication, their songs became ever more garbled and their behaviour ever more outrageous and childish. One evening, this culminated in Joby emptying a bag of crisps down Father's trouser-front and catching him a swinging blow in the fork with Mother's handbag.

I observed these goings on with my nose pressed hard against the pub window. The curtains were only partly drawn, and through the foliage of a large but sickly-looking geranium plant whose pot was filled with stubbed-out cigarette ends, I vainly tried attracting Mother's attention to get replenishments sent out. I often resorted to asking people entering the pub to pass on messages requesting top-ups on the lemonade and crisp front, but even this ploy seldom bore fruit. The three hours to closing time seemed interminable, and the boredom acute, added to which it could always be guaranteed that Father and Joby would be amongst the last to leave.

One incident imprinted itself indelibly on my young mind. It was the kind of evil night that would prompt the more pessimistic Christians to hurriedly consult blueprints of the Ark. The rain was fairly bucketing down. Mother and I were already in the car when Joby, wearing only a light sweater, staggered out of the pub door and stood in the middle of the road tunelessly wailing the chorus of a dirty song.

A few moments later Father lurched out, tripped, and grabbed Joby for support. He clung on desperately to the still caterwauling unidexter, before eventually slithering slowly to the ground. Pulled temporarily off balance, Joby collapsed on top of him and both lay in a bedraggled heap laughing uncontrollably until, managing to regain sufficient composure, they hauled themselves to their feet and stumbled to the car. Amazingly, as always, Father safely delivered Joby to his front door before driving unerringly home.

It wasn't always necessary for Father's little car trips to culminate in a visit to the pub for him to end up legless. He and Tom Draper had been pals in their youth back in the 1920s. They'd always kept loosely in touch, but hadn't actually seen each other for about fifteen years.

The trusty old Wolseley ground to a halt outside a quaint little stone cottage on the outskirts of Stourton. Rather strangely, it seemed to me, Tom and his wife were not cowering in the kitchen, or hurriedly effecting an exit through the back door, thinly disguised as visiting social workers. They actually greeted us warmly and ushered us into – their snug little living room. Its low, oak-beamed ceiling seemed to press down upon the clutter of heavy furniture and china ornaments. Fingers of pale winter sunlight picked their way through diamond-leaded lights and the foliage of numerous pot plants that jostled for position on the window-sill. A well-banked coal fire glowed in the grate and two massive tabby cats were curled up approvingly on the hearth rug absorbing most of its heat. It was the perfect picture of cosy domesticity.

Tom was, I estimated, perhaps a year or two older than Father. A wiry little man with a thin leathery face, bushy brows and darkly flashing, yet humorous eyes. He walked awkwardly on a game leg that had been badly wounded during the war. Conversely, his wife Bessie was large, robust and florid, with great wide hips that seemed to present her with something of a problem as she threaded her way through the closely packed furniture.

Sustained by lashings of tea and copious amounts of home-made walnut cake, the homely conversation traversed decades of nostalgia. The characters and events mentioned meant nothing to me, and as my mind quietly slipped away, the whole thread of their recollective dialogue became progessively more woolly, until eventually it was lost completely. Tom and Father suddenly downed their teacups and, rising from their chairs, headed towards the kitchen.

"Bring the boy if y' like," Tom said to Father.

Picking up on this, I followed them into the kitchen, intrigued to see what had warranted the sudden upheaval. As we wandered through the cottage my intrigue was quickly satiated. Bottles – everywhere bottles. The shelves in the kitchen sagged under their combined weight. The cupboard under the stairs was full to over-flowing. They stood on the twisting staircase and on many of the window-sills. The spare bedroom was crammed with them and even the bathroom could boast a couple of dozen or more. Filled with liquids of countless subtle hues, and bearing small paper labels proclaiming the likes of 'Elderberry '56', 'Rhubarb '57', 'Rose Hip '56', 'Nettle & Honey '55', and a host of other mystic runes, they were all the tangible evidence needed to tell us that Tom was a fanatical, and incredibly productive, home-made wine buff.

Naturally, it didn't take long before glasses were produced and the first bottle broached. As the afternoon gathered together the dusk of early evening, Tom periodically limped in clutching fresh armfuls of bottles for sampling and assessment.

"Plum this one, three years old. Nice an' round an' fruity!" he announced with obvious satisfaction, as he yet again filled Father's glass.

"Aye, a fairish drop o' jollop!" pronounced Father. "What's thik one there?" he queried, squinting hard at the label. "Says 1953, that ought t' blow yer 'at off I reckons!"

"That'll be a drop o' sloe!" said Tom with some pride. "Last o' the batch from thik year I thinks. 'Twill slide down a treat that will. One o' me better ones!"

And so they continued, manfully forging their way through 'Potato '55', 'Elderflower Champagne '57', 'Barley '57', 'Parsnip '54'; all the while becoming ever more relaxed and garrulous. Mother and Bessie, apart from one glass of Elderflower Champagne, had stuck wisely to cups of tea. At Tom's behest I had sampled three or four part glasses and already my eyelids were beginning to feel distinctly leaden. The conversation, aided and abetted by the alcohol, twisted and looped its way around a wide variety of subjects before Tom, who during the war had been in on the tail end of the North African Campaign and later fought his way up the spine of Italy, introduced a souring note.

"'Course!" he observed, twisting a glassful of 'Turnip '56' at eye level to examine the contents, "whilst we was out stickin' our boots up Jerry's arse you'd got yerself onto a nice little reserved occupation hadn't y'?"

"Wadda y' mean?" bristled Father. "Somebody 'ad t' produce the food t' feed you buggers!"

"Well yes, but you was safe enough on the land wasn't y'?" replied Tom.

"Safe be buggered," reacted Father, rearing up in his chair like a trodden upon ferret. "I wasn't sittin' round on me arse y'know. I was doin' me bit. In the 'ome guard I was. Us 'ad t' be out there. Guardin' Ilchester bridge we was. When us started out all I 'ad were a torch an' a nobbly nutstick. Our 'eadquarters were a bloody fowl 'ut down off the bridge on the river bank. I used t' stand out on thik bridge wi' they Jerry bombers dronin' over 'ead an' shake me nutstick up at 'em. 'Come down 'ere an' fight you buggers!' I did shout!"

"An' s'posin' they did!" said Tom.

"S'posin' they did what?" queried Father.

"Well s'posin' they came down t' fight!" replied Tom.

"Ah well, the sods couldn't could um? And if they 'ad I'd 'ave showed um a thing or two I'll tell thee!"

"'ow?" asked Tom beginning to get to Father. "S'posin' one o' they Jerry paratroopers 'ad've come sailin' down an' walked up t' thee brandishin' 'is cocked Schmeisser, just what would you 'ave done, stood standin' there wi' yer nobbly nutstick?"

"Dussn't thee worry," bragged Father, "I'd've sorted the bugger out an' no mistake!"

"Alright, c'mon, just what would you 'ave done?" pressed Tom.

"Well, fer a start," replied Father, beginning to look a trifle desperate, "If 'ed o' asked I the way I wouldn't o' told un,"

Tom and Bessie began to chuckle. The beginnings of a smile even fluttered momentarily across Mother's lips, but I wasn't convinced she knew exactly why.

"No, seriously," countered Father, earnestly intent upon keeping his credibility intact. "A little bit o' psychological warfare that is. Worse thing you can do to 'em. I reckons they'd rather be shot than 'ave that done to 'em. See, that's why, when they were expectin' the invasion, we turned all the signposts round!"

"Any road," he continued, beginning to feel firmer ground beneath his feet, "I knows you buggers might 'ave 'ad a bit o' lead flyin' about over there an' all that, but at least they fed thee well enough. I'll bet thees wasn't on short commons like we was over 'ere wi' the rationin'!"

"Rubbish!" retorted Tom. "Rationin' never 'it you lot out in the countryside. In the cities maybe, but I'll wager the likes o' thee didn't go wi'out!"

"Ah well, that's where you'm wrong," smiled Father triumphantly, "Cos I well remembers when war broke out us was livin' over t'Fifehead Magdalen, out Shaftesbury way, an' we used t' go t'Raisons the butchers over t' Marnhull, an' 'e used t' turn out some lovely rabbit pies. Caw! girt thick crusts on 'em, an' beautiful pastry 'twere, an' the fillin' – bloody girt succullent lumps o' prime rabbit, an' the juices. Caw! they were lovely, thick they were, beautiful! Thees couldn't turn out nuthin' like it could thee Gwen?"

Mother, forced to agree, shook her head dolefully.

"Then this 'ere bloody rationin' came in," Father continued "An' wha's think, they pies went right off. I went over t'see old Raison meself. "'Ere', I said, 'I'm buggered if thy pies ain't gone down'ill a bit of late!"

"Well," he said, "I knows, but see I just can't get the rabbits wi' all this 'ere bloody rationin' goin' on. Anybody nettin' a few now be keepin' 'em theirselves, or else slingin' 'em over the 'andle-bars o' their bikes an' takin' 'em off up t' Shaftesbury Market. One an' a tanner a time they be fetchin'. I tell thee I can't keep up sides wi' it! To tell thee the truth," he said, "between you an' me, I've bin forced to add a bit o' other meat to it, t' pad it out a bit thees knows!"

"'Ave y'" I said, "Like what?"

"A bit o' 'oss meat" he said, kind o' quiet like.

"Is that right?" I said, "Caw, an' I were thinkin' they pies were nowhere near s' toothsome as they used t' be neither!"

"'Tis alright," he said, "No rubbish goes in. 'Tis all fit fer 'uman consumption"

"Well, 'ow much be thees puttin' in?" I asked un.

"Well, d'vary, but the last batch, I reckon 'twere about 'alf an' 'alf!"

"Alf an' 'alf?" I said.

"Ah," 'er said, "About one rabbit t'one 'oss!"

There were a few moments of silence, Father remaining stony-faced and impassive, before Tom and Bessie, suddenly twigging his uncharacteristically subtle drollery, fairly fell about laughing. It was fully five minutes before they had completely regained their composure. Throughout, Mother had sat with a quizzical expression furrowing her brow, until eventually feeling moved to enquire, "Is that what 'appened to old Reg the greengrocers 'orse then?"

Well, they may have laughed at the original tale, but at this question, so obviously asked in all innocence, Tom and Bessie exploded. They literally rocked with mirth. Tom was at first bent double, then stretched full length, his head craned back over the head-rest of his armchair, mouth opened wide, uvula dancing merrily. Bessie was clutching her bosom and producing gales of laughter; cackling uncontrollably as tears ran down her face. Even Father had joined in with a volley of coarse guffaws. Mother sat quietly smirking, obviously delighted that she had been the font of so much merriment, but quite clearly unable to fathom why. The warm conviviality had returned, and the evening continued in hearty humour. With the two men broaching yet more bottles, and discussing the merits of Saddleback pigs, the warmth of the hearth on my face, and the languid ticking of a huge, brass-faced wall clock hypnotising my brain, I peacefully surrendered to sleep.

*With the two men broaching more bottles and discussing the
merits of Saddleback pigs I surrendered to sleep.*

A huge, gruff paw shaking my shoulder jolted me from my slumber.
"C'mon, it's nearly quarter t'twelve!" slurred Father's voice, in a tone
that suggested the passing time had all, somehow, been my fault.
My wits reassembled just as Bessie returned to the room bearing a
tray of two dozen home-produced eggs. Father was swaying dangerously and giggling inanely as he attempted the normally simple task
of putting on his overcoat. Both he and Tom were obviously much
the worse for drink. Plucking up a glass and swallowing one last
mouthful of 'Gooseberry '57', Father lurched unsteadily towards the
door.

"Gi' they eggs t' Toby. 'E can carry the buggers!" he gulped.

Stuffing a bottle of 'Elderberry '55' into his coat pocket, he shook
off Mother's steadying hand and staggered out into the night. We
reached the car, and Father slumped into the driving seat. Bidding
rowdy farewells, then, gunning the old Wolseley into life, we slewed
off down the road. Being sloshed on home-made wine was clearly
proving a different kettle-o'-fish to being sloshed on Ushers' Best
Bitter, and the car was deviating far more unnervingly than it had

ever done on its way home from the New Inn. Patches of fog were adding to his already considerable problems as we weaved our way erratically homeward. Numerous divots carved from the grass verges were strewn along our route and I struggled to balance the tray of eggs as I was thrown about the back seat.

We were within a mile of home when Father, approaching a familiar T-junction through thick fog, made his gross error of judgement. Assuming that at that time of night, and in thickening fog, no-one else would be using this quiet stretch of road, he failed to slacken speed. The haloed lights of a fast approaching car suddenly burst from the bank of fog on our right. Through an alcoholic haze Father reacted, and the Wolseley's jaded brake linings bit deep. As the other vehicle slewed past our nose, horn blaring, I was suddenly aware of my backside being no longer anchored to the rear seat. I shot forward bodily, at a marginally lower velocity than the tray of eggs I was holding. Continuing their headlong flight, thirty nourishing, free-range eggs peppered the inside of the windscreen, the dashboard, and the back of Father's trilby hat. If a single egg remained unbroken, we certainly never found it; and if a single glass of home-made wine ever again passed Father's lips, I certainly never witnessed it.

7.
Hormones, Earthworms
& Dirigibles

HORMONES HAD BROKEN IN under the cover of darkness, and even now were running amok throughout my whole being. I was lamentably unprepared for such a traumatic incursion. My voice was beginning to sound like the coarse gratings of a distressed magpie. Wiry hairs were sprouting alarmingly in the most outlandish places, and the face was erupting like a pan of Mother's gravy just coming to the boil. I was, to say the least, uneasy. My first reaction had been to watch the phases of the moon with uncustomary zeal quietly fearing the onset of chronic lycanthropy. Each time I caught a glimpse of my pickled features, I shrivelled. There seemed no way of overcoming the army of inflamed pustules that jostled for shoulder room on every inch of cheek and temple.

"You've been at it again," wailed Mother, "There's smear marks all over the bleedin' bathroom mirror!"

She was right of course, and although the resounding "Zblatt!" of purulent contents rifling from a prime zit and spattering the bevelled glass was somehow in itself satisfying, it did nothing to improve the overall picture. Never has a balaclava seemed so desirable. Maybe there was no great mystery to the Invisible Man after all. Just another desperate acne sufferer. Every waking hour my mind raced, searching for some way of disguising the disfigured gargoyle I now saw sitting atop my neck. Then, leaping out from the pages of the *Daily Mirror* one evening came my salvation. 'Medac – the improved treatment for acne sufferers – conceals as it heals' the advert confidently proclaimed. This was for me! I began badgering Mother to get me a tube. She was none too keen and obviously saw fit to mention it to Father. His observations were delivered with customary reassurance and even-handedness.

"Wha's up wi' you, turnin' into a bit of a jessy or summat? We'd

114

o' got chucked out o' the navy fer usin' bloody make-up!"

But, with even more weighty pestering, Mother eventually yielded, and upon returning home from the Saturday shopping trip, her bag disgorged the salvational pink and white box. I smuggled it surreptitiously into the bathroom. The instructions were clear enough it seemed: 'Squeeze small amount from tube onto offending blemish and carefully blend into surrounding skin area'. This presented me with something of a problem because virtually all of my 'surrounding skin area' was already occupied by yet further spots. However, after several ham-fisted attempts, I managed to create a passable mask of concealment. The ointment had, as its promotional blurb had claimed, hidden all but the most mortiferous eruptions. Its skin-toned colouring had blended perfectly with my flesh and so far as I could see was undetectable. I now sallied forth upon the world with a reborn confidence.

I couldn't help noticing that a few girls and one or two older women were eying me with obvious interest. It was fast becoming apparent that unfettered by my diced liver complexion I was, after all, quite attractive to the opposite sex. I was lifted, elated by the discovery, borne along on a cushion of well-being. I began to strut.

Buoyed still further by this burgeoning adolescent vanity, I consulted the rear view mirror of a parked delivery van just to check upon my evidently new found *beau-fatale*. I was mortified by what stared back at me. A hideous Mardi Gras mask in bright 'dayglow' pink. Suddenly, but one thought was uppermost in the mind of a creature who, moments before, had been strutting like an egocentric peacock, 'Where do I hide myself until the next bus home?' What I'd failed to realize in so carefully applying my camouflage beneath the bathroom's artificial light was that, when exposed to natural daylight, the 'Medac', so recently hurled into the bin, turned bright baby-pink and gave off an almost incandescent glow.

Fortunately for me, at this time, Linda Gregory must have detected something faintly redeeming amidst the pustules, lank hair and gangling ectomorphic frame. Or was it just that I offered a familiar, if erupting, face. I had known Linda years before – when I was about eight in fact, and she was a pupil at Heywood village school. She had been a terribly unconvincing Boadicea, teetering precariously on a rickety trolley pulled by two aging but good humoured goats, in the Coronation Fancy Dress parade. Her parents had recently moved to Wincanton and she now found herself once more, in the same school class as me. I liked to think that the bond between us was forged way back in those early days, when I was called upon to perform a particularly tricky operation upon Hector – her moth-eaten, but much revered, teddy bear. I had been the suave surgeon and she the practising anaesthetist.

Hector went out like a light.

Hector lay upon her Mother's ironing table and as I hovered over him with a handkerchief tied about my face, Linda, pouring a liberal measure from one of her Father's gin bottles onto a cloth pad, held it to Hector's nose. As an anaesthetic it proved to be very effective for Hector went out like a light. Using my pocket knife, carefully sterilized over the spout of a steaming kettle, I opened up his tiny abdomen with meticulous precision and probed around amidst the soft

116

stuffing with searching fingers. Ah yes! There it was, the little bounder, nestling there at the bottom of the thoracic cavity, the source of all Hector's problems.

Linda looked on apprehensively, dabbing my forehead a couple of times with a slightly greasy wiping up cloth. Deep concern for her threadbare little friend spread across her face. Ever so gingerly I eased the offending little box out through the incision and a deep sigh of relief escaped Linda's lips, playing warmly on my right ear. With cotton and a darning needle I adroitly sewed up the wound, leaving as neat a scar as one could wish to see. To my knowledge that had been the first successful abdominal squeakerotomy ever performed in the village. The memory of my illustrious deed had obviously stuck with her because it now became evident that she was keen for us to 'go to the pictures' together.

That Saturday evening, as I waited impatiently outside the local cinema for her arrival, my whole body was a matrix of jangling nerves. I'd never been called upon to do this before. It was a totally new departure in my life. Prizing the money out of Mother in the first place had been hero's work indeed, and I still wasn't sure I was going to have enough left for the bus fare home.

It was a chill, blustery evening and as I stood, collar raised against the whipping wind, hands thrust deep in pockets, moving my weight impatiently from foot to foot, I considered what demands might have to be met over the next few hours; and it wasn't the icy fingers of the wind that sent a violent shiver racing through my bones. A pugilistic old black and white Tom cat sauntered across the cinema forecourt. He paused momentarily, tail quivering aloft, to send a fine spray of pungent urine up a mock Doric column, before shambling past and casting me a worldly-wise look which said, 'Strewth, you won't catch me 'angin' abaht on freezin' cold pavements t' get my oats mate!'

There were flea pits and there were flea pits, and the Plaza would have most cheerfully fallen into either category. It was still recuperating from a recent showing of 'Rock around the Clock' during which one of the usherettes had her ice-cream tray ransacked and the majority of the ashtrays went A.W.O.L.

I hadn't really taken note of what the double feature offered, but I rather felt that it was all a bit incidental anyhow, as Linda had distinctly said, 'Get there early so that we can get a seat in the back row!' Naive as I was, I could still appreciate the portent of that instruction.

I was early alright, amongst the first. But where was she? Surely I wasn't going to be blown out on my first date. It was the spots. That was it – when it came to the crunch, she just couldn't face the spots. Panic and self doubt were beginning to mount alarmingly, when from around the corner, she suddenly appeared. As we entered the foyer I noticed she was wearing lipstick; she certainly looked considerably older than her thirteen years. I caught a faint whiff of heavy perfume too. Oh, I hoped I was going to be able to cope. All I had to call upon in this hour of direst need were a few vague playground mutterings and some very fundamental school biology lessons.

I approached the ticket kiosk in a dilatory manner, quietly hoping that she might offer to pay her half, still fearing my bus ride home was in jeopardy. But no. My four shillings and sixpence disappeared without trace, and my sixpence change, I knew, wouldn't count for very much at the interval. In the meantime, Linda had removed her top coat and I was able to appreciate that nature had been quite busy in the years since that pioneering squeakerotomy. Bumps and things were disturbingly evident beneath the thin woollen jumper and large, limpid brown eyes fluttered coquettishly. I could feel my throat drying up and the palms of my hands becoming suddenly moist. I could have sworn they'd just turned the foyer heating up by at least a dozen notches.

We crossed to the auditorium door, entered, and were immediately accosted by an arm with a torch on it. At the other end of the arm stood 'Tessa-the-tank' usherette – and for three years running, 'South Western Area All-in Barbed Wire Eating Champion'! She took the tickets from me and, with a threatening grunt, tore them theatrically in half.

Tessa wasn't tall, but she was built with something to spare. To describe her bosom as enormous would be to lay oneself open to accusations of belittlement. They hung about her frontage like two mighty dirigibles, moored to her clavicles, and enfolding the most commodious cleavage imaginable. This – so popular local legend had it – could be pressed into service in an emergency. If necessary she could abandon her floodlit tray and still carry with her enough choc-ices and soft drinks to keep the patrons happy during the interval. But Tessa's main claim to notoriety was in the use of her torch. Scores of young courting couples would testify that, just as the action in the back row was at its most hectic, they'd be suddenly illuminated by her well-directed beam. It was well accepted by all that, in accuracy of both timing and aim, Tessa was indeed a craftswoman *par excellence*.

Lighting our way along the rear aisle she led us to our seats and, giving us a knowing look, turned and left. I had the seat next to the aisle and Linda was sat to my right. The rest of the row was occupied by numerous other young couples, all obviously impatient for the lights to dim.

The moment the auditorium was pitched into darkness and the cockerel began crowing its lungs out to herald the start of the Pathe News, the sounds of bodies changing positions could be heard. Bumps, creaks, and rustlings were augmented by playful giggles and barely audible whisperings of 'Not yet!', 'Leave over will you!' and 'You're sitting on my toffees fathead!' I sat rigid, unsure of my next move. I glanced sideways at Linda. She was gazing straight ahead at the screen. Dry-mouthed, I waited a while until the main feature was well under way. I glanced at Linda again. Her eyes were still fixed to the silver screen watching Douglas Fairbanks Jnr, leaping about in gung-ho abandon and generally swashing his buckle.

I was beginning to sorely regret not having been more attentive in the few biology lessons we had received. Mind you, I lay the blame for my lamentable unpreparedness squarely at the door of old 'Adolf' Meyer, our science and biology master. I thought him a total waste of space. 'German', all the kids reckoned. In truth I believe he was of Viennese extraction, but having retained a distinct Teutonic accent he sounded German enough to the general hoi-polloi to warrant the epithet of 'Adolf'.

He was a slight, whippety, though rather dapper man, with slicked back hair, greying at the temples, and a tendency to flighty, nervous movement. His sunken, somewhat cadaverous face was dominated by a prominent hooked nose on which balanced a pair of small gold-rimmed spectacles. The mouth was narrow and mean, the eyes piercing, grey and humourless. I had not been amongst his favourite pupils, since Father had rather bewilderingly insisted upon attending an 'open day' shortly after my arrival at the school. My mind drifted back to that occasion. Father had chosen a packed assembly hall as his platform to hold forth on the subject of modern teaching methods. I stood some distance away, striving to look as inconspicuous as possible. "I don't 'old wi' teachin' all this 'ere science an' French an' rubbish!" he trumpeted "Don't do 'em a penn'orth o' good.

When's 'em goin' t'use it? You answer me that. They'll forget the lot soon as they've left. Waste o' bloody taxpayers' money. When I were a boy us did only 'ave readin', writin' an' sums, wi' per'aps a bit o' scripture chucked in. We did do alright on the strength of it. In fact I still got a prize at 'ome I won fer sums!"

Mr Meyer, who was standing nearby, unwisely saw fit to interject,

"Surely you must agree, zat in a modern society, havink der knowledge of scientific subjects und biology vill give zem vider 'orizons to take viz zem to ze outside vorld!"

"Oh ah?" replied Father, looking around to garner approbation from the gathering, "So you're the science master are you? An' I suppose," he continued, exhibiting commendable bigotry, "You'll be learnin' they little buggers 'ow t' build a doodlebug or summat will yer?"

Mr Meyer resisted rising to the bait, but he'd pigeon-holed the incident, and unfortunately for me, was fully aware of whose Father had just been addressing him. He was not a man to forgive lightly. In fairness, I must have sorely tried his patience in the science lab; I was, it seemed, simply incapable of grasping the subject. Whilst my classmates were conducting dramatic experiments with such heady substances as copper sulphate, litmus paper, and iron filings, I was still struggling manfully to master the fundamentals of the humble Bunsen burner. I just could not get the holes at the bottom adjusted correctly. The flame was either out, or searing the paint off the laboratory ceiling.

When marking items of written work old 'Adolf' had the habit of circling the mark he'd scribbled in the margin with a bold ring. Upon opening one piece of work just returned from marking, I noticed that the bold ring was in the margin as usual, but contained no mark. Vengefully thinking I might catch him out and put egg on his face in front of everyone, I hoisted my hand and blurted out across the class,

"Sir, you've forgotten to put a mark in the ring in my margin!"

There was a momentary pause as he smiled the smile that crocodiles smile just before amputating your leg.

"Dyer," he hissed, "had it not occured to you zat perhaps I have forgotten to put a ring around your mark?".

'Bang!' Shot with me own gun!

I fared somewhat better at basic biology. Seemingly, I was much more in tune with living organisms than with obscure crystals and things that mysteriously changed colour or bubbled meaninglessly along glass tubes. However, despite my interest in biology blossoming and my work attaining a reasonable standard, old 'Adolf' had not forgotton Father. I was totally unaware of this, until one afternoon we broached the subject of earthworms.

"Vot," quizzed 'Adolf', "can anyvun tell me about earz vermps?"

The usual sea of blank faces stared back at him. This, I felt was the great opportunity to redress some of my shortcomings in general science, for about earthworms I did know something. My right hand shot in the air, and I stretched forward waving my arm slightly, whilst my left hand supported it at the oxter. 'Adolf' ignored me for a while, obviously waiting for any other response that might be forthcoming. But the rest of the class sat there, a tapestry of ink, filth and snot, and moved not a muscle. Eventually, turning towards me, he announced,

"Very vell, Dyer vill now tell us all zat he knows about vermps!"

"Well fer a start," I gabbled, "If you cuts 'em in 'alf both 'alves live!"

"Hmmm!" he mused, grey eyes narrowing cruelly. "Not if you cut zem lenksvays!"

Still obviously nursing animosity, 'Adolf' even saw fit to make the recommendation to my form master that, academically, he considered me ideally suited to fill the vacant role of milk monitor – and I'm proud to say that by sheer hard work and perseverance I proved him right.

In recent months biology had taken on a faintly reproductive slant. Obviously it was the result of a dictate from higher echelons, as 'Adolf' looked distinctly reluctant to tread that path at all. He was perceptibly ill at ease when the male and female of anything were called upon to appear on his blackboard together. One rather suspected that had the 'Great Architect' seen fit to dispense with apples, serpents and spare ribs, and been content to people the world with self-seeding hermaphrodites, 'Adolf's life would have been cheered considerably. He covered the reproduction of the amoeba at great length, but I had to confess to finding some difficulty in relating this to the buzzing I felt in my ears when watching the fifth-year girls playing netball.

Our next sobering dip into the bran tub of sex education might be euphemistically termed as 'the birds and the bees'. Plenty of the former, and precious little of the latter. There was a brief film show covering the elaborate courting dance of the Great Crested Grebe, the lekking activities of the Scottish Black cock, and the male Puffin doing various endearing things with a beakful of sand eels. But I still failed to relate. Somehow I wasn't fully convinced that sitting my backside in the water and paddling at speed up the municipal boating lake, shuffling and genuflexing around some remote Highland conifer plantation, or gently nuzzling a nubile ear with a mouthful of Mevagissey Whitebait, was going to cut very much ice with the sceptical crumpet of Form 3A.

Added to this, 'Adolf's' verbal explanations of avian mating techniques were, I found, a trifle ambiguous, and if taken at face value by the more impressionable, could easily have led to a very frustrating fortnight on the back lawn with a chaffinch. When lecturing on such delicate subjects as 'naughty things going on in nature', 'Adolf' would perch atop a very tall stool, and with hooked nose, cold, piercing stare, and narrow hunched shoulders, he would look every bit the predatory goshawk impatient to slip the jesses.

With gimlet eye he surveyed the class, eager to spot any suggestion of knowing nudge or titter. But still he failed to grasp the 'sex educational' nettle, and his instructions became ever more vague and circuitous. Once, and only once did he touch upon the subject of rabbits. I was just beginning to relate their legendary fecundity to the basic adolescent urges that were presently running rife through my body when, for some obscure reason, he allowed himself to become sidetracked into parasites of the gut.

My reverie dissolved, and as my mind slowly returned to the cinema screen I realized that the main feature had moved on apace. However, it still seemed to be revolving around Douglas Fairbanks Jnr. having a surfeit of buckle which he seemed only too eager to swash about. He was, even now, swarming up the rigging of a captured corsair brigantine anchored somewhere off the coast of St. Kitts, and judging by the unsightly bulge in his theatrical tights, I reckoned that the motley assortment of salty sea-dogs manning the decks below might be well advised to keep their backs to the binnacle.

I glanced once more at Linda. She smiled warmly. Encouraged, I gulped apprehensively and slid my arm tentatively along the back of her seat. Her fragrant body melted slightly towards mine. My searching fingers found something round, warm and soft, and in the darkness I began to knead and fondle it gently. It was her shoulder – but it was a start – and it triggered me into trying to recall the exact sequence events should now take. My mind swept back over 'Adolf's' lectures in the desperate search for pointers. Without doubt his most comprehensive instruction had been on the amoeba. In consequence I sat for the rest of the main feature with my arm around Linda, patiently awaiting the first tell-tale signs of binary fission.

The film drew to its close predictably enough with the suave, clean-cut Douglas Fairbanks Jnr., padded codpiece still well to the fore, comprehensively putting one across those awfully sweaty, unshaven and skulduggerous freebooters. Single-handedly he had scourged them from the high seas, with the final score at 419 for 7 declared.

Pausing only to confirm that Linda was still in the singular, I excused myself and headed hotfoot for the 'gents'. My thoughts for the past hour and a half had not been solely upon things libidinous, and operation 'Safeguard a Sixpence' was now underway. Whatever the outcome of the evening, I found the prospect of a cold walk home less than compelling. My plan, with only sixpence left to my name, was one of monetary conservation. I'd disappear to the toilet just a bit sharpish, and then generally loiter about until such time as the interval was drawing to its close, and the titanic Tessa and her colleague had disappeared with their ice cream trays – thus avoiding the expenditure I could so ill-afford.

Unless unfortunate enough to have been struck down by a particularly violent attack of 'Bombay belly', it's a bit difficult padding out a public toilet visit to ten minutes. However, by casually changing stalls, and sidling quietly from one vacant cubicle to the next, I slowly reached my target. Content that I'd stretched it out for long enough, so to speak, I washed and dried my hands, and was standing in front of the mirror, about to attempt putting a racy quiff back into my wayward hair, when I received a nasty shock. Stone the crows! – was that merely a blemish on the mirror, or was that spot on the side of my nose one of the most impressive I'd ever seen? A great yellow throbbing thing it was, and I swear there was no sign of it when I'd left home. I knew all my spots individually and had the salient details of each mentally catalogued. This one had definitely not put in an appearance before. It was difficult to believe that anything quite so awesome could have seeded, flourished, and blossomed in the space of just two hours. How could it do this to me? On my very first date and all, and when I'd already been intimate with a shoulder.

I waited for the toilet to clear of bodies. Then, quick as a flash,

I brought the nails of both index fingers into play and, scurrying swiftly out, left the janitor to puzzle later over the smears on the mirror. With all the nonchalance I could muster in the wake of such a discovery, I sauntered back into the auditorium. But I'd mistimed it. 'Tessa-the-tank' was still at her post, tray at her waist, and gargantuan appendages concealing most of the merchandise. I stalled and dithered and, that was my undoing for, just as I was about to bolt back to 'Twyfords' sanctuary, Linda caught sight of me and smiled beckoningly – I was sunk. Upon reaching her, I was reluctantly about to enquire her pleasure, when she suddenly produced a bag of 'Butterkist' and offered me one – I was afloat again! As I retook my seat the cinema began to quake rythmically. Tessa was making the long trek back to the box office. Phew, that had indeed been a close one!

Pitched once more into darkness, I sat watching the opening credits of the 'B' feature Western, starring the likes of Rip Torn and Slim Pickins, whilst my wits were gathering about me a master plan to take my campaign a step further than Linda's shoulder. Without warning, matters were snatched from my hands. Leaning across Linda placed her arm behind my neck and drew me to her. The smell of her perfume was overpowering, flooding my brain; I became acutely aware of a fragment of 'Butterkist' still wedged between my teeth. Ever so gently she placed her warm yielding lips upon mine. She purred seductively, slowly increasing the pressure. I was conscious of not being exactly sure where to station my nose, as it was, I'd always been convinced, rather on the large side, and bound to get in the way. But all such thoughts gradually melted under the warmth of her urgent caress. After what seemed an eternity she relented and, drawing her face away slightly, whispered,

"There, that wasn't so bad was it?"

Gagging for air, I found it impossible to conjure up an answer on the spot. I also found it difficult to believe that this little siren was only thirteen-years-old. She certainly seemed to know the score, whereas I hadn't even read the rules. But there was no doubt about it, things they were a-changing. For suddenly the temples were pounding, the testosterone was on a tidal surge, and I was in musk. Grabbing her to me with all the subtlety of a Grizzly bear breaking into a bee-hive, I returned her kiss and, shunning the aid of a safety net, we locked in passionate embrace. Somewhere through a swirling pink haze I recalled the plan I'd so recently been hatching, to extend my familiarity one step beyond the shoulder.

Watchful for any signs of demur, I eased my hand gently beneath the waistband of her jumper, then slowly upward, fingers searching hither and thither for buttons and things. I encountered none until I was about four inches from her throat. Overcoming these left me confronted by a high-cut chemise and a heavily fortified bra.

I was in trouble and I knew it. My elbow was in her lap, my wrist at her throat, and my hand contorted at something more than right angles, fingers probing in vain at the perimeter defences of her undergarments. My neck was wryed at an impossible angle as I strove valiantly to maintain oral contact. All in all, I was slumped there giving a very passable impersonation of Richard III.

I was forced to admit it, I was stumped. I began wondering how Linda might be scoring these fumbling efforts on an imaginary scale of say, one to ten when, glancing along the row, I realised that most of the other young couples were already operating enthusiastically on a scale of 10 to 20 – and if I wasn't sorely mistaken that lad on the far end in the corduroy bomber jacket was already well into treble figures. My mind refocussed upon my own predicament. It had to be faced, I'd totally run out of ideas. My goal was tantalisingly just out of reach, and my wrist was beginning to ache. The inner me offered up a tiny prayer that 'Tessa-the-tank' would trundle into view brandishing her flashing torch and get me off the hook.

To this day I have never even begun to understand the mystifying powers of telepathy but, just as I was preparing to concede defeat by asking Linda if any more 'Butterkist' were left lurking in the bag, a shaft of light lanced along row 'R' and a score of writhing bodies were galvanised into the upright position. 'Saint Tessa's' timing had been uncanny, not only because she'd saved my proverbial bacon, but also because back on screen the cavalry had just arrived and were heroically cutting a bloody swathe through the tattered remnants of the Sioux nation.

I saw Linda to her front gate and was dismissed with a cursory cuddle. Her front door closed with a thud and the metallic rattle of a letterbox, leaving me alone with the night. Since earlier in the evening the wind had hardened from chill to bitter. I thrust my hand deep in my pocket, fumbling for the sixpence, so shrewdly conserved; remembered suddenly that the half fare had recently gone up to eightpence, and walked dejectedly home. My first tentative dip into sexual dalliance had been, by any standards, bankrupt.

Linda had now taken her attentions elsewhere, probably to someone whose knowledge of things procreative extended a little way beyond invertebrates. I had, however, learned one thing in the harsh university of life. A hazy knowledge of basic biology and the worldly art of pulling a bird were indeed horses of a very different colour.

Parental guidance upon anything as delicate and distasteful as the fundamental facts of life was assiduously avoided until one bleak January day, some four years later, on the windswept platform of Frome railway station. I was leaning out of a carriage window, bidding my parents farewell, as I embarked upon the journey northwards to Shrewsbury and army basic training. Mother was quietly piping her eye for general effect, and the stationmaster already whistling and flagging for the off, when Father felt moved to open his casket of homespun sexual philosophy for the first and only time. Just one priceless pearl escaped, "An' if thees' gets theeself a sprog, don't bring the bugger back 'ere."

9.
Dogma, Toenails & Raspberry Jam

TAKEN BY AND LARGE, basic table manners and Father were mutually exclusive. He was, without question, a stolid trencherman; but with taste buds atrophied by years of exposure to Mother's appalling litany of culinary disasters, he now looked upon meals not so much as something to be savoured, but more as a means of topping up on essential fuels. Almost without exception, Mother's savoury meals were silted up with heavy coatings of glutinous gravy, and her sweets were submerged beneath a sea of lumpy custard. Brimming over the edge, they tended to form cold stagnant puddles on the already stained tablecloth.

Watching Father raise and tilt his plate to let the dregs dribble into his mouth, wipe a cuff across his chin and summon up a gaseous belch, I somehow instinctively felt that I was witnessing a coach and horses being driven through some of the finer social graces. In time honoured tradition, tea was poured into the saucer to cool before drinking. When sucking it from the rim, Father always contrived to produce the evocative sound of fine shingle being hauled back down a steep beach by the tidal undertow. But possibly the most disarming aspect was his obvious delight in giving exaggerated displays of these foot-in-the-trough manners to any poor soul unfortunate enough to find themselves visiting the house at mealtimes. In particular he'd relish the prospect of disgusting anyone he considered to be relatively more socially advantaged than himself.

So it was with Mrs Rowena Layzell, a well spoken, kindly, and cultured lady, wife of a retired naval Commander, and welfare visitor for the Royal Naval Association. Within the framework of this 'association', retired naval officers and their wives paid visits to ex-Naval 'other ranks' who were either retired from their civilian occupations or were in generally low paid employment. Their aim was to keep a weather eye on their circumstances and lend a charitable hand should it ever be required. Father's twelve years spent shovelling coal into the boilers of some of His Majesty's less august warships, allied to his presently dismal agricultural wage had, it seemed, qualified him admirably for their kindred vigilance. A cosy and well meaning organisation, it had in Mrs Layzell a charming, diligent and ever-helpful worker who had, so to speak, drawn one of life's short straws.

This particular 'short straw' outwardly resented the implication that it was in any way of lowly means, and would welcome her with surly reticence and a churlish desire to belittle all her efforts. Although persevering with commendable resolve, she singularly failed to win Father's co-operation. He seemed totally unprepared, or perhaps unable, to bestride the socio-economic schism he perceived between them.

On the one hand sat Father – gruff, fundamentally uncouth, with dog-ends wedged behind his ears, and cowshit all over his boots, entrenched knee-deep in his trite socialist dogma which, at any given opportunity, he was prepared to spit out with all the ill-considered venom of a malevolent wildcat cornered in a crofter's privy. Whilst on the other sat Mrs Layzell, the cultured product of a private education – punctilious, immaculately coiffured, eminently socially advantaged and, I would imagine, standing politically somewhere just to the right of Genghis Khan. There seemed little enough common ground, and Father seemed intent on laying waste to what little there was. But, to her eternal credit, Mrs Layzell was not a woman to be discouraged. She swept in one Sunday teatime and in her precise, clipped tones cheerily announced,

"Strawberries Mr Dyer, I've brought you some delicious fresh strawberries."

"Strawberries?" replied Father disbelievingly, "'Tis only the middle o' soddin' April!"

"I know,' she smiled condescendingly, "but we do have our little contacts don't we, and I thought they'd make a nice little treat for you and Mrs Dyer!"

"Ah well they might for 'er," he answered sourly, "but I'm 'appy enough 'ere wi' me bit o' cold rabbit an' a few spuds. Anyhow, they'll be they bloody force cultivated things I'll warrant. Voreign muck I shouldn't be 'alf surprised. No taste, no smell, an' bugger all good t' man nor beast!"

"Well, you just try them and see what you think!" rejoined Mrs Layzell, refusing to be ruffled.

"An' I s'pose you'll be wantin' a cup o' tea now you're 'ere!" Father observed dourly.

"Oh yes. Splendid. Love one. Thank you!" she gushed enthusiastically.

"Ah, I guessed as much!"

"Oh, and by the way," she added, "just to round them off I've brought a lovely tub of dairy cream. Really scrumptious eh?"

"Scrumptious?" groaned Father looking distinctly dismayed, "bloody 'orrible more like!"

"What's the matter, don't you want any cream?" Mrs Layzell enquired.

"No, I'm buggered if I do!" he growled. "An' if thees' 'auled on as many cows tits as I 'ave in my time, thees wouldn't want none neither!!"

Mrs Layzell winced slightly as her mind wrestled with the images, and Father's face took on a wolfish look. He'd spotted the first chink in her armour, and from now on would subtly exploit her susceptibilities. On each of her subsequent visits he tested her mettle further. I watched, almost in disbelief, as his displays became increasingly boorish and distasteful in both word and deed. He was obviously relishing the spectacle of her recoiling from his tasteless vulgarity.

Raspberry jam was the straw that finally broke the camel's back. Making an almost superhuman effort to appease and placate, Mrs Layzell arrived on one of her many Sunday tea-time visits and, thrusting a paper bag into Mother's arms announced,

"Scones, freshly baked this very morning, and what else but a jar of homemade raspberry jam'"

"Oh!" said Mother, "You shouldn't 'ave, you're very good to us. You must take on a few sticks o' rhubarb!"

"Ah I thought I 'eard your car!" bellowed Father, appearing suddenly at the back door. "Bit o' success t'day look!" he grinned, holding up a couple of extremely lifeless moles. "They buggers won't be 'eavin' up me onion sets no more!"

Mrs Layzell clasped her hand to her mouth to cover a sharp intake of breath – and Father smiled quietly to himself as he kicked off his muddied gardening boots.

Striding to the kitchen table, he pulled out a chair, sat down, and broke wind with earth trembling force. Mrs Layzell turned her head away and momentarily closed her eyes, as her face registered total disgust. Father beamed triumphantly.

"Onions!" he proclaimed, "Roar through thee system like a set o' drain rods they do!"

"'Ere, wha's got there Gwen?"

"Mrs Layzell 'ave bought some scones for tea, an' some 'ome made jam!" Mother replied.

"Caw! bugger me! Well don't 'ang about, get it on the table woman!" he instructed. As the atmosphere slowly lost some of its sulphurous taint, tea was hastily laid and Father was in amongst the scones and jam with a vengeance.

After a while he began sucking exaggeratedly at his top palate,

"Caw!" he said "I reckons I've got a couple o' bloody raspberry pips wedged under me top plate!"

So saying he placed his fingers in his mouth and withdrew his top set. Inspecting them briefly, he dunked them in his cup of tea and began swilling them around vigorously. Satisfied, he shook off the surplus tea and popped them back in his mouth. Picking up a teaspoon he clumsily fished a couple of pips from the surface of his tea and deposited them on the side of his plate.

"'Ere that's better!" he said, "I'm damned if they little buggers don't play up!"

Mrs Layzell watched open-mouthed as he then poured his tea into the saucer in preparation for his seashore impressions. Shaking her head, she pushed her plate away and rose from the table, saying,

"I do apologise but I must be going, there are a couple of other visits I wish to make this evening!" Grabbing her jacket, she continued, "I'll pop in some time next week, or the week after!"

Contrary to her assurance, she never did 'pop in' the following week nor any week following that. It was the last we ever saw of her. Barnyard etiquette had triumphed over good intention, and Father was quietly content.

Even when not consciously trying, Father still possessed the gift of being pretty obnoxious. Indeed, this was so graphically illustrated one Saturday teatime when a recently made pal of mine, Ken Bates, was invited to stay for a bite to eat.

At fifteen years of age there is a tendancy to be ultra-sensitive about the impressions you're making upon your peers, and I must admit that knowing Father's track record, I had felt distinctly uneasy as Mother had asked Ken to join us at the food table. My angst was to prove well founded. As Mother busied herself setting the table and cobbling together the bloater paste and limp lettuce sandwiches, Ken and I watched uncomfortably as Father crouched intently over the newspaper, ear cocked to the wireless, scribbling down the football results, and picking his nose with a demonic fervour. We had just learned that Cowdenbeath had notched up a comfortable away victory over Stenhousemuir when Father, experiencing obvious difficulties with one particularly recalcitrant bogey, hastily tore away a part sheet from his newspaper, blew his nose lustily into it, and, screwing it into a loose ball, cast it backhandedly towards the fire. As it dropped about three feet short and pitched onto the rag-mat, Ken glanced towards me with a distinctly queasy look about his face.

"Right, sit in!" directed Mother, as the sturdy pine table creaked under the weight of one of her homemade 'fairy' spongecakes. The meal was proving generally uneventful, with Ken manfully tackling the daunting stack of bloater-paste sandwiches, and Father, having surmounted his acute nasal blockage, choosing to ignore us as he checked the results against his coupon. Uneventful, that was, until Mother chose to ask,

"Another cup o'tea Ken?"

Desperate for something with which to wash down the surfeit of fish paste sarnies now clogging his craw, he replied with alacrity,

"Yes please!"

"One sugar wasn't it?" queried Mother.

"Yes, that's right, one!" he confirmed.

Stirring the tea vigorously she handed it to him.

As I recall we both spotted it simultaneously. There, eddying around on the surface of Ken's tea, was a large, yellowish – grey crescent of toe-nail. Smiling weakly he recoiled, looking even more green about the gills than he had done previously. I deduced in a moment how it had got there. Every other Friday was bath night for Father; and the previous evening, having silted up the overflow, he had sat before the fire clipping his toe-nails. As always, the clippings had been whizzing about, ricochetting off various surfaces like so much stray shrapnel. This one, judging by its size and thickness, coming from one of his big toes, had obviously shot into the sugar bowl and buried itself from view. There it had lain, undetected, until Mother had unwittingly transferred it to Ken's cup with the spoonful of sugar.

"Ummm, there appears to be a toe-nail in Ken's tea!" I announced.

"Where?" croaked Father, suddenly setting aside his pools coupon and taking notice.

"There, look, floatin' around on the top!"

"Bugger me so 'tis. Must be one o' mine!" he observed pulling the cup and saucer towards him and studying it with a frown.

"Wonder 'ow that got there?" he mused, picking up a teaspoon and chasing the offending horny crescent around the rim of the cup. Eventually outwitting it, he fished it out, and deposited it on the saucer.

"Well, if 'tis this week's 'twill be fresh enough an' no mistake!" he chortled tastelessly. Then, with a final admiring glance at it, he pushed the cup and saucer back towards a disbelieving Ken, saying, "There y'are m'boy, that's sorted that out for y'. Good as new, get it down y'!"

But Mother quickly interceded.

"Frank!" she scolded, "You can't expect the boy t' drink it like that!"

Ken gave a lame smile of relief, obviously thankful for the timely rescue.

"For 'eavens sake where's your common manners?" Mother continued. "Hook that disgusting toe-nail off 'is saucer!"

I think it was that evening, after Ken had fled, that I devised my long term plan of escape. I'd already been pilloried by Father on the subject of further education when announcing that we were having to decide what subjects to pursue for GCE's.

"None!" he barked, "Thee's don't wanna bide an' waste thee time caddlin' wi' thik rubbish, 'twon't do thee an ap'orths worth o' good. Thee's wanna get thee arse out there an' rake some coinage into the family pot! I did never 'ave no fancy cerstificuts when I wur at schoolin', an' nobody can say it did I a blind bit o' 'arm!"

I was by no means convinced that khaki was in any way up my street sartorially, but a spell with the County Regiment seemed the ideal way out.

10.
Axes, Ostriches
& Slogger-Holes

ALTHOUGH A FIVE YEAR SPELL in the army had given me a temporary reprieve from Father's 'university of questionable social graces', I found myself, upon discharge from my unit, almost involuntarily sucked back into the fold. I had decided to pursue a 'civvy street' career as an Inspector with the RSPCA. Upon being accepted, I discovered that there was a six months' waiting period before the commencement of the next probationary class. It thus became evident that I needed both lodgings and a job to tide me over. At that time the family effects, having been disgorged yet again from the insides of a foul smelling cattle lorry, were huddled beneath the less than weatherproof slates of a farm cottage at Longbridge Deverill, and it was here that I was welcomed home with an unnerving enthusiasm.

I was uneasy. Two world wars, the Depression and the much lamented demolition of the Lamb Brewery had failed to change Father, so why the past five years? I found myself constantly alert to any signs of reversion to type. Reassuringly, they were not long in coming, and life once more assumed its old predictable pattern. The village of Longbridge Deverill was only a metaphorical 'stones throw' from Longleat, and it was upon Longleat Estate that I was to find temporary employment. Taken on as a forestry hand, I found myself joining a 'gang' comprised of local lads on short-term employment like myself, and a few old stalwarts who were indeed true men of the woods.

In retrospect I consider myself truly fortunate to have spent that six months toiling beneath the emerald mantle of Longleat's woods. We used not a single mechanical tool; only axe, slasher, bille and brush hook.

The work was physical and arduous, the sweat and blisters on unhardened hands both profuse and painful, but the work place was idyllic. The senses were invaded as though by drinking a honeydew of intoxication. Nostrils were filled with the smell of crushed wild garlic, damp leaf mould and decaying wood. Capricious sylvan breezes stirred the leaves from their languor and created dancing pools of dappled sunlight upon the woodland floor. Bird song was everywhere as tiny feathered throats vibrated their territorial challenge, punctuated at intervals by the hollow ring of steel on sycamore, the anguished sigh of rending heartwood and the splash of a toppled tree breaking through the outstretched arms of an arboreal neighbour. I was filled by a sense of being at one with all things about me.

I had joined the 'gang' in the middle of 'thinning'. Beech plantations, some thirty or so years old, had been invaded by other would-be colonists, mainly ash, sycamore, birch and hazel. These had to be felled to enable the valuable beech to prosper. Chain-saws were shunned; the axe was the tool for the job, and the 'old stalwarts' were the men for the job. Their technique and efficiency were far and away superior to we younger, supposedly fitter, pretenders.

Clem Gray, our sixty year old 'ganger', weighed in at about nine stones of taut, wiry sinew. Dark Romany eyes, exuding all the vulpine cunning of an old dog fox picking the padlock on a henhouse door, twinkled beneath heavily bushed brows. His weathered face, with the texture of an old hiking boot, carried an ever-present wry grin as it peered out from beneath a battered old trilby hat which retained only half its brim. His wit was quick and dry, his observations uncannily perceptive and often disconcerting. His knowledge was deep and his woodland skills manifold. He could put an edge on an axe that would cleanly shave the hairs from your arm, and with the next breath identify the droppings of any animal found in the woods, by rolling them between finger and thumb and gently sniffing their odour.

He lived in one of the woodland cottages, and about its kitchen beams hung cured hams, not of pork, but of badger. He was the last man I ever knew who ate badger meat. One rainy lunchtime he offered me a badger sandwich from his lunch-box. To me it tasted remarkably like pork. To this day I couldn't swear that it wasn't. But that was the enigmatic nature of the man.

Clem's 'second-in-command' was totally the opposite in almost every respect. Max Hurley was younger, perhaps in his early forties. He was low, slow, and lugubrious, at times verging on the obtuse. Not that anyone would have seen fit to make this observation to his face, for Max was best described as huge. Six-feet-five, or maybe six, he towered way above us all. Max's most notable feature was his apparent lack of shoulders. From beneath the ears his neck thickened dramatically like the bole of a venerable chestnut tree. It was not fat, but solid muscle and at its base it seemed to simply blend into a cylindrical, relatively slight upper torso, showing no perceptible horizontal aspects where one would expect to find the shoulders. In relation, his head seemed absurdly small and his two enormously muscular and powerful arms gave the impression of sprouting directly from his neck.

His trousers were cut more than generously about his crotch, and he wore them hauled up high with his belt about his lower chest. This served to give the impression of long legs, a rather large abdomen, rather paltry upper torso, huge neck, tiny head and massive arms. Caught in certain lights he often reminded me of prints I'd seen of selectively bred strains of Old English fighting cocks. In description Max might sound ungainly and awkward but put an axe in his hand, step back and witness poetry.

We were felling ash and sycamore of anything up to almost a foot in diameter, and Max, with his seven pound axe, honed to an edge that could be confidently employed in neurosurgery, was dropping them on a sixpence with seldom more than half-a-dozen mighty blows. Whereas we lesser arboreal mortals, with our puny five-pounders, were delivering at least three times as many blows and scattering in panic as they toppled in all directions.

Max was certainly not one given to histrionic humour, but was a man of few carefully chosen words who was steeped in the lore of the woods. I was to discover this during the lunch-break of my third day. Aching in every sinew, I sprawled gratefully onto the bosky turve, my head resting wearily on my lunch bag. The sunlight was pleasantly warm, and as the soft sounds of the wood permeated my brain, I closed my eyes and began to drift. I was suddenly aware, as the insides of my eyelids turned from bright vermillion to sombre burgundy, that some huge bulk was cutting off the sunlight. I looked up to see the megalithic outline of Max hovering over me. As I hauled myself up onto my elbows he began to address me, stumbling awkwardly over his words.

'I d' 'spec' thee's bin wonderin' why we d' never shout 'Timber 'in th' 'ood. Well," he continued in slow measured monotones, "'Tis 'cos we d' take it fer granted that if anythin' d'vall on thee 'ead 'twill be a tree."

As I grappled vainly for some apt riposte, he turned and, without registering the slightest change of expression, ambled gawkishly away.

Max lived with his widowed Mother in a tiny cottage in the estate village of Horningsham. His only form of transport was a very aged Excelsior motor-cycle combination. All three were a familiar sight to the shoppers in Warminster most Saturday mornings. The 'combination' was in a very lowly state of repair indeed. Few nuts and bolts were used where a length of twisted wire would do the job. The seat could no longer boast either covering or padding, but was now just a triangular framework of rusted springs. Oil leaked everywhere. All that remained of the original sidecar was the bottom frame to which Max had lashed, with copious amounts of wire, one extremely large fishbox. The fishbox was normally employed in carrying tools, peasticks, hay for the goat and other rustic paraphernalia; but on Saturday mornings, should the weather be the least bit clement, it carried his Mother.

Max, motorcycling gear consisting of one ex-Army greatcoat extra large, a leather flying helmet, a pair of goggles and a fine pair of despatch-rider's gauntlets, would sit astride his ramshackle steed. His mother, a homely little pepperpot of a woman, clad in a loud houndstooth overcoat and mauve felt hat tied on tightly with a floral headscarf, sat beside him on a cushion in the fishbox. Kicking the bike into life, and with his Mother grim-faced and white-knuck-led, desperately clutching her shopping bag to her lap, Max set off ahead of a pall of blue smoke, at a steady thirty miles an hour through the twisting country lanes.

For all his size and strength Max was really a great big pussy-cat who was very close to, and caring about his old Mother. This helped to explain why he, along with many others in the area, viewed the introduction of exotic animals in general, and lions in particular, onto the estate with a great deal of uneasiness. He confided that he had often entertained visions of his mother being silently stalked by a slinking tawny form as she made her way home from the village shop, or pounced upon and consumed in one sitting whilst dead-heading her Sweet Williams. In the event it wasn't lions, but ostriches, that were to make their presence felt in the neighbourhood. Three – or was it four – we heard had escaped from their enclosure and had, thus far, avoided recapture.

The odd village inebriate rolling home from the Bath Arms had lain claim to glimpsing one, but by and large, for such a vast and leggy creature, they were keeping a pretty low profile.

At about half-past six one Tuesday morning, responding to his Mother's request, Max headed out of the cottage back door with a plateful of assorted scraps for the birds. He was only a few strides from the door when he pulled up short. There, standing on the lawn, only feet from the bird table, peering at him with jaundiced eye through the hazy half-light, was one of the fugitive ostriches. Max turned not a hair, and walking calmly back into the kitchen, placed the scraps down upon the draining board,

"Ere, Mother!" he said confidingly, his face betraying not a hint of humour, "I reckons thee's be overfeedin' they sparrers a touch!"

"Ere Mother, I reckons thee's be overfeedin' they sparrers a touch!"

Although slow of tongue Max could be quicksilver of hand. It was often difficult to fathom exactly why he was being doubly productive whilst seemingly expending half the effort. True, his prodigious strength came into play when wielding an axe, but not when using the bille or brush hook. Preparation of his tools must have played a big part. Hone as I might I couldn't get my axe to cleanly dry shave my arm. Amazingly Max's could perform this feat after felling a half a dozen fair-sized trees. To my regret, I never did learn his secret.

Technique was probably the primary factor in his efficacy. Like all good countrymen, he had the uncanny knack of allowing his chosen tool to do all the work. One hot August day we were set to the perennially unpopular task of 'flat-trimming'.

We were stood atop a gentle slope, and surveying with some dismay countless hundreds of regimented little conifers, all about two feet high. Most of them looked in imminent danger of being overwhelmed by a verdant tangle of bramble, bracken and willow herb. Our task, a particularly unappetising one on so hot a day, was to trim away the offending undergrowth with brush hooks allowing them room to flourish. As we started, I was a couple of rows to the right of Max, and shouted across to him,

"A bit odd workin' down 'ill ain't it? It wouldn't be so far t'stoop workin' up the slope!"

"Aye, s'pose yer right m'boy," he replied. "But us've allus worked down at 'ill on these 'ere bit!"

So saying he bent his long back and began reaping the bracken with practised ease. For a moment I watched, and compared his action to that of others of my own ilk. They were hacking furiously and expending great effort in hauling the cut growth clear of the trees. In contrast Max was using his brush hook with minimal movement of the upper arm and a smooth sweeping movement of the wrist.

There was need to cover the ground quickly as we were on 'piecework', but there was also need to exercise care, as each severed sapling would cost us ls.6d. One or two of us, in vainly hoping to deceive, attempted wedging toppled saplings back into the soil hoping to avoid detection; but old Clem, the 'ganger' with the all-seeing eye of a scavenging buzzard, promptly strode across and kicked them over. The late morning heat was searing on the open hillside and the horseflies had discovered that we'd blood in our veins. Sweat poured from my brow, my mouth was parched and my back and forearm ached with a vengeance.

"Right! Time for a bit o' nunch!" hollered Clem.

His words were music, and as I eased myself upright, quietly swearing that I'd never again decorate a bloody Christmas tree, I peered down the slope to see just how far ahead Max had got. There he was, about thirty yards ahead, still operating as smoothly and effortlessly as ever and determined to clear just a couple more yards before breaking off. Old Clem hailed him once more.

"Max! Nunch time!"

Max raised his brush hook in acknowledgement and, through the shimmering heat haze, began trudging back up the hill. When he reached us I could see that, despite his apparently effortless style, Max was fairly lathered in sweat and looking decidedly cerise about the gills. I was puzzled as to why, in the circumstances, he was still wearing a light woollen jumper beneath tightly buttoned weskit.

"'Ow can you bear t'wear all those togs on a day like this?" I asked him.

He took a long swig from his bottle of cold tea and considered the question for a moment, before hitting me smack between the eyes with a statement of the purest country logic,

"What keps th' cold out'll kep the 'eat out!"

I was left to ponder this as we once more took up our brush hooks. I glanced down the slope and there was Max, who'd forged on ahead, already bent to his task. Buckling down for another stint I almost immediately miscued and lopped off a tree. Grabbing it, I quickly jammed it into the ground, saw Clem advancing purposefully towards me, and kicked it over myself.

Suddenly the air was rent by a distressed wail,

"Yaaarghh!!"

It had emanated from the bottom of the slope. All eyes turned to where the hitherto six-feet-five-inch Max had now apparently shrunk to about four-feet-nine. Dropping our tools and hurdling bracken and briar, we charged headlong down the slope towards the stricken figure. Max had fallen into a 'slogger-hole', and there he stood up to his thighs in oozing mud.

Perfidious things, slogger-holes. Looking solid enough with their lushly grassed surfaces, they ensnare the unwary by yielding almost instantly when trodden upon, and this one had certainly outwitted Max. He stood there looking forlorn, turning his head slowly from side to side as he took in the geography of the feature. As he was so often wont to do when about to make a profound statement, he tugged his cap around his head so that the peak sat above his right ear. Adopting the quaintly bemused expression of an orphaned wildebeest he began to enunciate with a slow matter-of-factness.

"Ere, wha's think, if I remembers rightly, I vell in 'ere last year!"

11.
Ceilidhs, Sly sows
& Soup du Jour

IT WAS WHILST WORKING at Longleat that a weekend trip to Swangage brought about my meeting with Rachel, the girl who was eventually to become my wife. She hailed from just outside Glasgow, but as a trainee veterinary nurse was presently employed in Swanage. She shared a terraced house in one of the quieter streets with two other girls, also trainee veterinary nurses.

On the day in question I was casually ambling past the town's pitch-n-putt course, my mind focused on nothing in particular, when a rather aged looking Jack Russell tore across the pavement in front of me. It shot out into the busy road, neatly sidestepping a couple of cars and two expansively-beamed ladies on a tandem, before steaming up the hill, around the corner and out of sight. Moments later a rather flustered young lady appeared, moving at the extended trot. Bringing my stunted mathematical brain into play I quickly deduced the sum of two and two.

"Lost a little brown an' white dog 'ave you?" I asked.

"Oh!-Ya!" she replied in a very non-Dorset accent. "Ist fur my friend's dog, and from me she ist suddenly runnink. Are you seeing what road she ist goink?"

"Yes!" I said, "Up the 'ill an' round the corner. Don't panic, leave it to me!" I assured her. "I'll catch it for y'!"

So saying I was off like a ferret down a rabbit hole. Full of youthful enthusiasm and long-legged athletisism I gave chase. But in catching alarmed Jack Russells I was long on gallantry but woefully short on technique. In fact I only glimpsed the infernal thing once. Just its hindmost six inches as it disappeared through the base of a privet hedge. After a while I conceded. Somewhat crestfallen I made my way back towards the anxious young lady whom I had by now left some distance behind. To preserve a rather fragile young male ego I toyed with the idea of fabricating a tale of crocodile wrestling in the town's millpond, but thought better of it.

"No luck I'm afraid, she was too quick for me," I informed her with commendable honesty, "Shot through a hedge an' disappeared!"

"Oh not to be worryink," she smiled weakly, "I go fetching my friend, she help me look some more. Ya?"

"Ya!" I assured her, "I'll just keep lookin' around. We'd best meet up somewhere to see if we've 'ad any luck. You know where the amusement arcade is on the front do you?"

She nodded.

"Alright, I'll meet you there, at say, four o'clock. OK?"

"Ya! Ist no problem. See you there. By the vay, my name ist Inga!"

"Oh, right!" I replied, "Just call me Toby!"

With that she was gone. At four o'clock I arrived outside the amusement arcade, having given up the fruitless search more than half an hour earlier. For about ten minutes I stood in the pulsating wave of sound that emanated from within, before Inga appeared with her friend.

"It O.K!" she beamed, "When I get back to house, Ginty already there, find own way home before me. Zis my friend Rachel, she come viz me, say 'sankyou' for trying to find Ginty!"

Tall, elegant, with flowing brunette hair and huge doe-like brown eyes, to describe Rachel merely as beautiful would be to dismiss the Taj Mahal as a gravestone. A large wooden mallet fell from the skies and struck me a stunning blow between the eyes. Gawping and gulping I desperately searched for some simple words with which to embark upon elemental conversation, but they had fled and hurriedly gone to ground. I stood totally thunderstruck!

"Perhaps ve shall go for a coffee someplace?" I heard Inga say from somewhere down a very long and echoing corridor.

"Yes!" some strange detached voice affirmed as my lips moved.

The one thing that my swimming brain seemed to register was that Rachel's accent was also something other than broad Dorset and somehow, in my heightened state of confusion, I managed to deduce that both she and Inga were Swedish.

We reached a cafe, ordered coffees, and I bumbled desperately for something to say, but my tongue had become wooden. Eventually, stumbling by chance across a few brain cells that were still operating normally, I managed to dredge up a relevant news item I'd recently read somewhere. Addressing Rachel, and hoping to impress, I burbled,

"I believe you've just changed over to driving on the left. Not you personally, that is – Uhm. In your country I mean – they've just changed over to driving on the other side – uhm, like we do in this country – on the left!"

"Have we?" she replied with puzzled expression, "I thought we'd always driven on the left!"

"Oh no!" I blundered on, "They really have just done it, in the last two or three weeks!" Hoping to salvage the situation a little I quipped, "I expect they'll change over the cars and motor-cycles now just to see how it goes, and change the lorries and buses over in three months time!"

Reaction – nil! However, there was no doubting it, for me, this represented the beginnings of the big romance. For Rachel it represented a very average cup of coffee and a thoroughly disjointed conversation with a bumbling idiot. Despite double-bogeying the first hole, I persevered doggedly over the ensuing weeks and months, learned that Inga was Swiss, Rachel was Scottish, and that indeed, allowing for the odd Burns' night aberration, motorists had never negotiated Kingussie High Street on the right-hand side. Eventually, worn down by sheer mulish persistence, Rachel relented and a relationship blossomed.

I put off taking her home to meet my parents for as long as possible, but eventually the day of reckoning arrived. It was a Sunday, and we were to face all that Mother could throw at us for both dinner and tea. I had forewarned Rachel of what to expect, but sensed that she was still woefully unprepared.

Father's welcome proved to be about as warm and reassuring as a slap around the face with a wet halibut. However, apart from that, his manner for the rest of the day was uncharacteristically subdued and undemonstrative. On the other hand, Mother scurried around enthusiastically, making gentle contented clucking sounds as she dished up some of her most inedible fare onto the least chipped china. A battle of wills ensued as she served up Father's tea in a cup – minus the saucer. Realizing her motive, he glared at her balefully, but she glared back, clenching her dentures and projecting her bottom lip. Father, resisting the urge to remonstrate, drank it down with a face as sour as a pickled walnut.

The day passed tediously, but without incident. In the evening I ferried Rachel back to Swanage, relieved that she had escaped the first encounter so lightly. I eventually arrived back home at about a quarter-to-one in the morning to find that the downstairs lights were, unexpectedly, still on. I cautiously entered the living room to find both Mother and Father still sitting up patiently waiting for the cat to come in so that they could throw it out for the night. Father leaned forwards in his chair and prodded the poker into a dying fire with some purpose, sending a shower of impish sparks scurrying up the chimney.

"Where the 'ell you bin?" he enquired sourly, "Thought thees were never comin' 'ome. Us bin sittin' 'ere in front o' these 'ere fire, starin' at they dyin' embryos, wonderin' where thees got to!"

Choosing to dismiss his bile, I asked eagerly,

"Well! What d'you think of 'er then?"

"She's very pretty!" observed Mother, "An' seems like a nice quiet girl!"

"Aha!" said Father raising a cautionary finger as he prepared to take Shakespeare to the cleaners, "Thees mark my words. 'Tis the sly sow that drinks most wash!"

"An' what's that supposed to mean?" I asked

"'Tis a quote from somebody hysterical!" he snapped, "An' it'd pay thee t'take 'eed, 'cos my old Dad used t'say that when 'e were alive, an 'e lived to be nearly ninety!"

I was suitably chastened but, despite Father's dire augury, I continued in amorous pursuit. Over the next couple of years the relationship flourished and eventually the prospect of marriage reared its head, as it's so often capable of doing.

Rachel's Father, a gaunt, sibilating man of sepulchral charm, completely wrong-footed us by greeting the news with an unexpected effusiveness. Neither of us had anticipated that he – an elder in the Kirk of Scotland and avid afficionado of Rabbie Burns – would welcome a mere Sassenach, and a relatively godless one at that, into his family fold with such apparent enthusiasm. Events were then rather wrenched from our hands as he initiated a campaign to propel his daughter towards the altar with the kind of indecent haste usually associated with mistimed withdrawals and cocked fowling pieces being brandished in the church vestibule.

There seemed to be some unspoken understanding between Rachel and me concerning the attendance of my parents at the wedding. We discussed all other aspects in depth, but both gratefully pussy-footed around the periphery of this burning question. Eventually, however, we took the proverbial bull by the horns and sat down to discuss it. We both felt that, fundamentally, it would be only right that they should be present at the marriage of their only begotten son, who for so long had filled the void in their life created by their inability to aquire 'a really good cow-dog'. However, in a more practical light, we could envisage Father being let loose amongst Rachel's very straight-laced and pious relatives and family friends. We quailed at the very prospect. We were faced with the dilemma of doing that which was morally right and Christian or that which was shamefully weak-kneed but, in the circumstances, prudent. In about ten seconds flat prudence and the wobbly patella had won by a unanimous points decision.

"It's a long and very tiring journey at your ages!" I advised, as I made it known to Mother and Father that the wedding was to be in Scotland. "And now you've given up the car you'll 'ave one devil of a job gettin' there anyhow!"

"Cor! Bugger me!" replied Father, "Us 'ouldn't miss that 'ould us Gwen? There's bound t'be a bit o' a do adderwards I s'pose. Us 'ad some scotch blokes on board ship in the Med, an' I'm buggered if they couldn't 'alf sink the ale!"

"A bit churchy, Rachel's lot actually," I informed him with all the tact I could muster, "Not really into swillin' beer an' singin' filthy songs!"

But Father's enthusiasm would not be dampened.

"Oh I'll soon cheer they buggers up don't thee worry. I ain't 'eard a hymn yet I can't drown wi' me gobbo'; an' dussn't thee worry thee-self overly about us gettin' up there, us'll go be coach, Royal Blue or Greyhound or summat!"

It wasn't looking good and, unbeknown to me, events were at that moment conspiring even further against me for, extending a warm, if misguided hand of friendship, Rachel's Father had written to my parents offering to accommodate them beneath his own roof for the duration of their stay. It was folly, pure folly. I knew instinctively that within the first twenty-four hours Father would have rendered himself about as welcome as an esurient mongoose in a snake-charmer's basket. However, the invitation had effectively shot my already threadbare argument down in flames and we had to accept, with the greatest trepidation, that Father would be at the wedding.

Three days before the wedding Rachel and I travelled up to Scotland to assist with the final preparations. The following evening I drove my van down to Glasgow bus station where Mother and Father were due to disembark at the end of their epic journey. As the coach trundled in Father spotted me and set about attracting my attention by dementedly thrashing the window with a rolled-up newspaper. The coach ground to a halt. The doors opened and a stream of weary looking passengers tumbled out. Mother and Father appeared near the tail-end of the exodus. Father was wearing a broad, self-satisfied grin as he barged unceremoniously past two elderly ladies who had paused momentarily at the bottom of the steps, sending one of them spinning in a full 360° pirouette. Looking dark-eyed and frail, Mother tripped along behind him in her anxious, pattering, shrew-like gait.

"Good trip?" I enquired, feeling somehow uneasy at Father's palpable bonhomie.

"Fair t' middlin,' I s'pose. Us 'ad t'change at Preston, but us managed t'grab a cup o' tea an' a bite t'eat, so 'tweren't too bad!"

"You look a bit whacked Mum!" I observed.

"Oh 'e wears me out sometimes, proper 'e does. All the way up 'e's bin entertainin' the other passengers. Y'know what 'e's like!"

I knew only too well; and as the words died on her lips, a middle-aged couple, trailing a half-asleep little girl by the hand, alighted untidily from the coach and glared darkly in our direction. Following closely behind came a slightly older couple. They too glowered pointedly at us, and suddenly I was transported back to those childhood seaside outings, with the insides shrivelling violently.

"You 'aven't!" I hissed accusingly. "You 'aven't brought that bloody mouth-organ!"

"'E 'as!" whined Mother, confirming my worst fears.

Father beamed, revealing the three gaps in his ill-serviced dentures and patted his breast pocket reassuringly.

"Right!" I said, lifting an admonishing finger, "You leave that bugger where it is. If I as much as catch a glimpse of it out of your pocket this weekend I'll 'ave it out of your 'and so fast it'll fair take the tread off yer finger tips!"

Father recoiled and scowled defensively. I collected their suitcases, and together we trailed out of the bus station and approached my parked van. I flung the suitcases in the back, and Father started to help Mother clamber in behind them.

"Ain't you lettin' Mother sit in the front?" I asked.

"Good suitcases them!" he replied. "She's a damn sight lighter than I be, she won't do 'alf as much damage sittin' on the buggers!"

With that he gave Mother one final shove and slammed the doors behind her. With Mother, Father and Rachel staying with Rachel's parents, the sleeping capacity at the house was filled, and I was relegated to a dingy little boarding house in East Kilbride. Its proprietress was a crab-faced, humourless old woman who, I swear, had lost three and sixpence betting on the outcome of Culloden. Her tongue was sharp and acid, the furry trimmings of her aged slippers appeared to be the victims of chronic eczema, and she was the part owner of a scrofulous, one-eared tomcat, with a snotty nose, that insisted upon jumping on your lap at the breakfast table each morning and sneezing all over your porridge. She had but one redeeming feature – she was cheap!

On the day prior to the wedding, I drove Father into Glasgow for a bit of a look around and a drink. We passed quite a few pubs by before Father eventually plumped for a particularly seedy looking establishment. We paid for our pints and made our way past the silent juke box and disabled pin-ball machine to a vacant table at the far side of the bar. Once seated, Father took up his glass and guzzled noisily before leaning back in his chair and appraising his surroundings.

"I likes this!" he eventually announced, wiping the froth from his chops with the back of his hand. "Sort o' like pubs used to be before the war. None o' these 'ere uppity airs an' graces an' fancy fittin's. I d'find that fancy fittin's generally means fancy prices!"

I was watching Father's pint shrinking at an alarming rate and silently lamenting that it was my round next, when the bar was suddenly invaded by half-a-dozen leather-clad bikers. They were of the beetle-browed, sloping-forehead, spider's-web-tattooed-about-the-jugular variety. As they clutched their pints and, with simian gait, slouched down the bar towards us, there was the disquieting sound of knuckles dragging on bare boards. They adopted a table nearby, turning chairs around so that they affectedly sat astride the seats the wrong way round slouching forward onto the chair backs. As I sat and watched, I found myself quietly questioning Charles Darwin's wisdom in risking scurvy, storm and tempest to sail all the way to the Galapagos, when ample evidence for the compilation of his *Origin of Species* could be found right here, communicating in primitive monosyllabic grunts and clutching pints of 'heavy'.

Within moments the juke-box had been liberally plied with small change and the bar reverberated to a medley of heavy rock and blues. A set of darts had been produced from behind the bar and two of the 'primitives' were hurling them at the dart-board with very limited accuracy. Father fell silent and sat observing them, stroking his chin ruefully. I headed back to the bar to recharge our glasses and turned to see Father bearing down upon the two dart hurlers. Without as much as a by-your-leave he grabbed the darts from the fist of one of them and launched into both lecture and demonstration.

"Thees'll never drow consistent darts the way you'm be carryin' on at it. You'm standin' too square-on be 'alf. Get thee drowin' voot vorwards an' cast thee weight onto the ball o' it! Lean in towards the board an' flight the darts wi' yer fingertips. You'm buggers looks as if you'm tryin' t' drow bricks drew a jeweller's shop window!"

He proceeded to demonstrate his point by throwing three darts top and two double tops, then, collecting them rather theatrically from the board, repeating the demonstration – top, double top and, for variety, treble nineteen. Open-mouthed, totally lost for words and each looking disturbingly like the archetypal portrayal of the missing link between the ape and the amoeba, the two bikers gawped at Father disbelievingly. I couldn't help noticing that the taller of the two was a digital amputee, having lost the little finger of his right hand. I was given to reflecting how, as the result, the statement crudely tattooed across his knuckles had somehow lost much of its impact – LOVE & HAT was calculated to intimidate no-one!

"I think you've done enough coachin' for one day!" I shouted to him above the blare of the juke-box, fearing that the bridge of his nose might be about to become the recipient of a 'Sauchiehall kiss'. His eyes fell upon his replenished glass and, without comment, he followed it, puppy-like, back to our table.

"Are you trying to steer considerable physical harm our way?" I asked him.

"Wad'ya mean?" he responded challengingly.

"What I mean is, that this is not some quiet rural pub in a Somerset backwater, and these are not your normal, muddle-headed drinking cronies. In Glasgow you don't just wander up t'blokes like those and start throwin' uncalled-for advice around!"

"But they was bloody clueless!" he insisted, raising his voice in self-justification.

"That's as maybe," I continued through clenched teeth, "but has it not struck you that they may not be the types that would be best pleased to 'ave you pointin' that out to 'em?"

Father subsided, and there were a few moments when I could see cogs and flywheels spinning furiously behind his disgruntled facade.

Without a word he rose suddenly from his seat.

"Where are you off to?" I challenged above the pounding din.

"Just goin' t'get some fags!" he replied, rummaging deeply in his trouser pockets for some elusive pieces of small change.

On his way back from the bar I saw him pause for a moment, and hover in front of the juke-box. Rejoining me, he took a deep draught from his glass, watching the six 'leatherclads' still raucously flipping beer mats in the air, blowing froth at each other, belching histrionically and generally rehearsing their bit-parts for the next blockbusting David Attenborough natural history series.

The seemingly endless round of rock music blaring from the jukebox suddenly gave way to the scarcely less offensive sound of Jimmy Shand's Accordian Band performing a bouncy little rendition of the Bluebell Polka. The 'primitives' fell silent, the last airborne beermat fell to the floor unheeded, each one gazed blankly as though being in receipt of a telling blow from a well-aimed blunt instrument. They stared briefly at each other, momentarily uncomprehending, before six pairs of eyes, burning with malice, focused squarely upon us.

"That was you!" I hissed accusingly, "You stuck that on didn't you?"

"'Twere the only 'alf decent thing I could see on there. At least it's a break from that other bloody racket!"

I shot a hasty glance back towards the twelve glowering eyes. Menace hung tangibly in the air. I was sure that at any moment one, or perhaps all of the 'primitives', would make some move, like drumming the chest and dashing about wildly, or chittering uncontrollably whilst tearing up sundry clumps of vegetation.

"Look!" I growled, "so far you are making all the right moves to ensure that tomorrow's wedding ceremony is consigned to a hospital ward. Get the rest o' that beer down y'. We're off!"

"I fancies another one!" he barked defiantly. "An' I ain't about t'let a bunch o' scruff-arses like that lot interfere wi' my pint!"

"I'm nippin' t' the toilet," I said, "Just sit there an' don't move a muscle. If you even feel like breathing, resist it!"

I returned to find him at the bar paying for another pint.

"Would o' got you one!" he said over his shoulder, "But y'don't seem t' 'ave the stummick fer it!"

Heavy 'rock' now pounded out once more, and the air of menace seemed to have abated somewhat.

"Right, c'mon 'urry up an' get it down yer neck," I said testily, "an' we'll get out of 'ere a bit sharpish before you upsets any more apple carts!"

Father was just draining his glass to order when the strains of Jimmy Shand's Accordian Band once more filled the bar.

"I just slipped t'other side on!" he announced with a triumphant grin. We left hurriedly.

Preparing to return to my dingy digs that night I said to Mother and Father, "Don't forget, tomorrow in Church, you're on the right 'and side, right down at the front!"

"Alright!" acknowledged Mother, "I'll make sure 'e washes 'is neck proper!"

I looked into her eyes, expecting to detect just a twinkle of humour; there was none.

"Dussn't thee worry theeself, we'll do our bit t'make sure 'tis a day nobody'll ferget in a 'urry!" assured Father, as an evil, self-satisfied grin wreathed his chops. I'd seen that grin many times before and it boded ill – that night I slept fitfully!

I rose at about half-past seven, pulled aside the discoloured net curtain and opened the bedroom window to examine the weather prospects for my big day. The sun was filtering weakly through hazy cloud like torchlight through a woolly hat, and an Arctic-spawned wind probed through my tee-shirt like an icy lance thrusting its way to my very vitals. Well, at least it was dry.

I peered into the dressing table mirror. The angry red zit on the side of my nose had burgeoned considerably overnight, ensuring its place in posterity as it appeared on every wedding photograph. Cursing my luck, I quickly slipped into a shirt and jeans and break-fasted without appetite.

Ken, my best man, and veteran of the dreaded 'toe-nail incident', arrived shortly afterwards and, under his scrutiny, I got togged up in my brand new C & A, off-the-peg, replica Savile Row 'Flareline' suit. Packing the rest of my traps in a suitcase and throwing it into the boot of Ken's car, I ventured down the hallway to settle with my saturnine landlady.

"Three nights at five pounds, that's fifteen pounds!" she deduced by furtive reference to her fingers. "There were two phone-calls as well, we'll call that sixteen pounds!"

"We'll call that fifteen pounds ten!" I said, "I haven't been ringing the speakin' clock in Honolulu!"

Grudgingly, she agreed.

"Looks like it's goin' t' stay fine for the wedding!" I said airily, hoping to lighten her mood somewhat.

"Didn't for mine!" she answered sourly, plugging in her iron and throwing a cotton vest onto the ironing-board.

On the way out I took a detour into the sitting room, where the one-eared tom-cat was taking his ease upon the arm of the sofa. I stroked his head and charitably assured him that I'd forgiven his nasal transgressions onto my porridge. He stretched his neck upwards to meet my hand, and sneezed violently, lacing the front of my suit with tendrils of silvery snot. I withdrew my charity and left.

At the church, Ken and I were ushered into the vestry by the Reverend Lindsay. He sat, quietly reminding us of the order of the ceremony, before clearing his throat slightly and announcing, a trifle self-consciously, in fairly broad Glaswegian,

"You'll eh, have noticed the floral decorations in the Kirk, and eh, the organist's music that eh, you requested, has been found with eh, no little difficulty by Mr McLellan the eh, Chief Elder. There exists a custom in the Kirk that the eh, Groom makes a small contribution towards his troubles. Eh, we normally recommend a sum eh, commensurate with the beauty of the Bride!"

"I don't carry that amount of money around with me!" I answered chivalrously. "Ow about a sum commensurate with the beauty of the Bride's Mother?" so saying I teasingly proffered a sixpenny piece. Reverend Lindsay took it and studied it thoughtfully for a moment, before replying with an impish twinkle dancing in his eye,

"See me after the ceremony Mr Dyer, you'll be eh, wanting your fivepence change!"

It wasn't whether or not Rachel would be late, or whether Ken had mislaid the ring, nor even that I might fumble my lines that was preoccupying my mind at this time, but what effect, if any, Father was having upon the day. I excused myself and made a little sortee out into the church. I spotted him standing there, second row back, exactly where he should be, and looking presentably tidy. I heaved a quiet sigh of relief. As I approached him, however, I saw he was wearing his silly grin. Moments later I sniffed his breath – my worst fears were confirmed!

"'Ad a couple o' snorts o' navy rum at some bugger's 'ouse afor we came!" he announced, as his feet became entangled with a hassock.

"No idea who 't were but by God they couldn't 'alf fill a glass!"

Oh, the fool, the misguided fool! Whoever it was had mistaken Father for a kindly sixty-five-year-old, who was just about to bask in his only son's biggest day, and had hospitably given him an innocent celebratory drink. Little did they realize that Father was, in fact, a highly volatile social grenade, packed to the gunnels with obnoxious tendencies, and by plying him with alcohol they had effectively removed his pin. He could go off at any moment.

Thankfully the church service went without incident, although I did discover later that, when first finding his seat, Father had to be reminded by one of the 'Elders' that smoking wasn't really acceptable in the house of God. Grunting something unintelligible, he had apparently stubbed it out on the back of the pew in front and stuck its remains behind his ear. In fairness though, it must be pointed out that Father was not a church-going man. He'd never been one to be over-impressed by omnipotence.

Once outside the Church we had to thank an eagle-eyed photographer for partly rescuing the Bride and Groom's parents' photograph, by spotting that Father was still wearing his cloth cap. Reluctantly, Father removed it, but later examination of the prints revealed it rolled tightly and sticking untidily out of his jacket pocket. No-one at all had spotted the scrawny dog-end still jauntily perched behind his ear.

Lightly as we may have escaped at the Church, the reception was to prove a veritable minefield. It was to be held at a rather superior East Kilbride hotel, noted for its lavish reception room and jealously guarded reputation for *haute-cuisine*. To follow the sit-down wedding breakfast, Rachel's parents had planned a ceilidh in the good old Scottish tradition. As Father had earlier earmarked it as 'a bit of a knees-up', I had already resigned myself to spending at least a percentage of my evening attempting to confine his boorish behaviour to within some kind of acceptable parameters. With his veins already laced with alcohol, the troubles started almost as soon as we sat down to eat.

"'Ere!" he shouted after one of the young waitresses, "Thees got any recipe?" She stared at him blankly.

"Menu!" I said, leaning across and attempting to clarify, "He means menu!"

"Oh!" she replied, "Not a written menu, no Sir, but I can tell you the choice of starters if you wish. There's melon!"

"No!" replied Father, dismissively.

"Or there's prawn cocktail!"

"What, a glassful o' lettuce wi' a spoonful o' pink jollop? Not bloody likely my girl!" he said, his face registering theatrical disgust.

"Wouldn't touch it wi' a soddin' yard brush!"

"Or there's the soup-du-jour!"

"Ah, that's more like it, I'll settle fer a drop o' that!"

Minutes later the same girl returned with Father's starter and, pausing for a moment whilst he removed his baccy box from his place setting, deposited it in front of him. He stared at it for long seconds before, picking up his dessert spoon, he began stirring it suspiciously, eventually fishing out a single pasta star.

"What the 'ells this then?" he bellowed."

"Italian vegetable soup Sir!" replied the alarmed girl.

"But I ordered soup-du-jour!"

"That is the soup-du-jour Sir!"

"Rubbish!" barked Father quickly loosing his rag. "A slip o' a wench like you tryin' t' teach yer Granny t' suck eggs? Us 'ad soup-du-jour at a British Legion do a couple of months back. Soup-du-jour's chicken, you ought t' know that, an' the proper stuff's got they little fried cretins floatin' about on the top!"

The poor girl looked mortified and I quickly interceded on her behalf.

"Look, d'you want the soup or not?"

"No I'm buggered if I can stummick thik voriegn muck!" he retorted, "I'll wait 'til the proper grub comes up!"

"What y' goin' t'ave then, turkey or beef?" I asked.

"Well, as 'tain't bloody Chris'mas we'm celebratin', I'll go fer the beef!" he grinned, obviously considering that he'd just delivered a telling shaft of wit.

"Right, put 'im down for beef for the main course would you!" I instructed the non-plussed waitress. "I'll 'ave 'is soup!"

Father was already getting very familiar with the wine bottle and, as I knew he couldn't handle wine, I whisked it away from him at the first opportunity and poured its contents into other glasses. However, another bottle found its way along the table and Father ambushed it like a praying mantis. He was going to show me up, I knew it; but perhaps the most galling factor was, so did he. Father's main course was brought by a rather dapper young man in a bow tie and maroon waistcoat.

"Wha's this bloody stuff?" he bellowed, picking up a slice of beef on his fork and waving it intimidatingly under the waiter's nose.

"Roast topside Sir!" the young man replied, matter-of-factly.

"Roast? Call this roast?" bristled Father indignantly, still waving the slice about on the end of his fork, "I likes my meat cooked proper!"

"The Chef has a preference for serving it slightly pink Sir!" advised the waiter with admirable aplomb.

"Pink? Wha's mean pink?" snapped Father, beginning to turn that self-same colour about the gills, "Bloody nigh-on raw more like it! I reckons an 'alf-decent vet'd 'ave this back on its veet in no time!"

"I'll see if I can arrange to have some of the more well-done pieces cut for Sir!" the lad offered steadfastly, before effecting an orderly withdrawal.

"An' some gravy, lets 'ave some proper gravy wi' a bit o' body in it!" Father hollered after him.

As most of the eyes in the hall were now focused upon him, I leaned over towards Father, "Have you got t'make such a damned song an' dance about everything?" I hissed from the corner of my mouth.

"Well," he slurred, draining his glass of yet another measure of Peter Dominic Leibfraumilch, "I ain't travelled all this way t'get palmed off wi' a load o' rubbish I can't eat!"

"If there's any more complaining t'do, I'll do it, understood?" I replied tersely.

"Oh ah? An' a fat lot o' good that'll do me an' all!" he moaned, "I still ain't 'ad me chicken soup!"

There was a blessed respite as he eagerly devoured his main-course, replenished, at length, with slices of well-cooked beef. However, the gravy, smooth and retaining its capacity for fluid movement, was still not to his liking. The young girl, so embarrassingly compromised over the starters, returned tentatively with the sweet trolley. Father, through alcoholic haze, recalled how, years earlier, he had so effectively ruffled Mrs Layzell's feathers with his ill-chosen comments about 'cream, and the pulling of cows tits', and thought that there might be some perverse merit in trying the same tack again.

"Don't dish I up any o' thik fancy stuff wi' cream on it. I can't stand cream!" he chortled wickedly, laying back in his chair and hooking his thumbs in his braces. "An' you wouldn't want cream neither if you'd pulled as many cows –" The words died on his lips. The girl had turned away and was attending to Rachel's Mother.

"'Ere!" he said, grabbing clumsily at the girl's arm, "I said I didn't want no cream, an' if you'd –"

"Sorry Sir, I'll be with you in a moment!" the girl replied, courteously but coldly. The moment had flown and, thankfully, Father knew it.

"Have you got to make such a song and dance about everything?"

I don't know whether or not true ceilidhs are meant to be spontaneous affairs, with individuals turning up with instruments and headfuls of songs and entertaining as the mood takes them, but what followed was organised by Rachel's Father with metronome precision. Two family friends played oboe and flute delightfully to piano accompaniment. No sooner had they finished than Rachel's Father, accompanied by the suspiciously effeminate looking pianist, took centre stage. With one hand resting on the piano top and the other about his diaphragm he stood, ramrod, and delivered a tremulous baritone rendition of 'Only A Rose' which, in places, sounded discordantly at odds with the piano. He continued by doing great disservice to a couple of obscure light operatic pieces, before finishing with a performance of 'Danny Boy' that would have had deceased Celtic patriarchs squirming in their graves. Father, sitting in the thick of Rachel's family and friends, was heard to comment all too loudly,

"Strewth! I'm buggered if I goes much on thik racket. Dear, oh dear! Sounds like a bloody cow calvin', straight it do!"

A couple of dozen faces turned towards him in unison. Each registered downright disgust and open hostility, excepting that of

Rachel's Uncle Jimmy, who had also partaken rather too freely of the nectar. "Aye, you're right!" he grinned at Father, "I've bin tellin' the man for years he cannae sing, but still he insists on gettin' up an' makin' a fool o' hisel'!" His refreshing honesty was rewarded by a sharp, admonishing 'Jimmy!' from his shrewish wife, and once more the family ranks closed.

Father was, by now, topping up his intake of Navy rum and wine with copious amounts of MacEwans bitter, and I felt torn between creating a scene by stepping in and hauling him, kicking and swearing, from the thick of it, or just leaving him in the hope that he'd run out of ideas and, responding to the frosty reception he was receiving, temper his behaviour somewhat. I lamely chose the latter course. It was a mistake.

The teeth-jarringly off-key performance of Rachel's Father was immediately followed by her Brother, Duncan, playing classical guitar and giving very polished performances of 'Fur Elise', 'Romanza' and a couple of other haunting pieces of that ilk.

"Caw!" remarked Father, as Duncan drew to a close, "'Er wasn't 'alf bad was 'er. I thought 'e could only strum the bugger!"

I watched as a strange phenomenon took place. There was no perceptible movement amongst the guests and yet, before my eyes, a vacant area was created around Father, leaving him isolated. For a brief moment I thought it might be as a result of Father's normal bodily reaction to the intake of too much rich food, but quickly realized that had this been so, they would have moved with far greater urgency. One or two amongst their number may have been magnanimous enough to forgive an old man, even my Father, for celebrating his only son's marriage by over-indulging in drink and becoming offensively loquacious, even if their kin were the targets of his acid tongue. However, in barracking a selection of recitations from Burns he served to alienate himself irrevocably.

The recitations were given by one Ewan MacGilp, a short, fat, balding, repugnant toad of a man. His eyes were of the shifty variety, and a pendulous dewlap of fat hung from beneath a weak receding chin. He had a soft, pink, sweaty palm, that I was once unfortunate enough to clasp in handshake, and he smelled faintly of mothballs. He was the current auxilliary kirk organ pumper and – so rumour would have it – the practising parish pederast. I had exercised my veto when I spotted his name on the guest-list but he had somehow slipped through.

He was selecting snippets hither and thither, and delivering them with a histrionic fervour, persperation beading his upper lip. For some reason the guests – Burns-afficionados to a man – were enraptured by his performance. I had to admit to finding him more than a touch tedious, and Father was getting dangerously restive.

The repulsive Ewan had been hogging centre-stage for a good twenty minutes and had just launched into "Ooooh wad some Pow'r the giftie gie us/ To see oursel's as others see us/ It would frae mony a blunder free us," when Father's tissue-thin tolerance gave way with a vengeance. "Oh fer cryin' out loud!" he bawled, "What a load o' bloody tripe. For Christ's sake put a sock in it, an' let's 'ave summat a bit more cheerful!"

It was a bad moment, things had plunged to their nadir, and I was forced to pounce.

"I could get the buggers goin' wi' me gobbo!" he protested as I grabbed him roughly by the arm and steered him towards more neutral ground.

"You could not!" I growled, "I don't know where you've got that thing 'idden but give it 'ere right now!"

"No!" he scowled petulantly, twisting away.

With the assorted works of Burns completed, the structured ceilidh gave way to a more normal wedding party with dancing and a few silly games. Much to my delight, Father seemed to have responded to my admonishment by going into his shell a bit and forming an even closer relationship with his pint glass. I did, however, observe him employing choice Chaucerian vernacular whilst tenaciously locking antlers with one of the guests over some vexed political issue or other; and he did manage to pitch Rachel's maiden Aunt – a practising Deaconess no less – into a state of the vapours, by offering his cack-handed congratulations upon her ending up with the rather tawdry set of six EPNS dessert forks I'd donated to be wrapped for 'pass-the-parcel'.

"All thees needs now," he observed, placing an arm a little too familiarly about her shoulders, "is t' ferget thee fancy, 'igh falutin ways, an' get theesel' a bloody good man!"

These two incidents apart, the next couple of hours passed relatively uneventfully. There was, however, to be a sting in the tail. At around 9.30 pm two groups of friends prepared to leave. Gordon, his wife and children were heading north to Oban, where they'd booked at a hotel as the first stage of a week's tour of the Highlands. On the other hand Glyn and his wife were heading south to their home near Buxton. Gordon soon had his brood organised, and I accompanied them to the car park where, in seconds flat, they were all packed into their tiny car, which wheezed asthmatically under the weight of a grossly overladen roof-rack. They tooted and waved optimistically as the little motor crawled unenthusiastically out of the gates and, with one last shuddering cough, disappeared into the night.

At that moment Glyn appeared at my shoulder. He was full of news and enthusiasm about his love of the Pennines and his recent adventures as a member of one of the 'Peak District Mountain Rescue' teams. He was particularly thrilled that the Alsatian he'd raised from a pup had just been enlisted onto the team. We tentatively arranged a weekend when Rachel and I might visit and experience a spot of fell walking around Bleaklow and Kinder Scout. Twenty minutes had flown by before the tail-lights of Glyn's car disappeared up the road, and I turned to re-enter the hotel.

As I crossed the foyer, my mind toying with images of peat-hag and curlew amongst the high peaks, I became suddenly aware of a distinctly metallic-sounding percussion invading my ears. A disarmingly familiar percussion, accompanied by a raucous, uncouth voice redolent of a cattle market. Fingers of steel gripped my entrails and twisted them into a tight knot. Someone had opened Pandora's box, and my most chilling nightmare had become reality. Slurred lyrics gradually became discernable.

"Cats on the roof-tops, Cats on the tiles!" the voice bawled, roughly to the tune of 'D'y' ken John Peel'.

"Cats with the clap an' the crabs an' the piles!" it continued tastelessly.

Suddenly galvanised, I swarmed up the staircase leading to the first floor reception area, was just negotiating the first bend three steps at a time when the next line hit me,

"Cats with their arse-'oles wreathed in smiles."

I'd just reached the top and was tearing headlong down the corridor when the vulgar little ditty was rounded off with,

"As they revel in the throes of fornication!"

I skidded to a halt and was confronted by a distraught and furious Rachel. Looking beyond her I could see most of the guests lain waste by Father's artless vaudeville.

"Where on earth have you been?" she screamed, suddenly abandoning what little compsure she had managed to retain against all the odds.

"The last ten minutes have been nothing short of awful. It's all Ken and Graham's fault. They egged him on, they knew what he was like. Poor Aunt Cath, a right state she's in, almost passed out twice!"

"Yes, he does tend to 'ave that effect on the more sensitive!" I replied conciliatorily.

"Well, get him under control!" she demanded flatly.

Father stood in time-honoured pose, balanced on a table, 'gobbo' and beertray clutched in hand. As I watched, the elfin figure of Mother tugged imploringly at his trouser leg in an attempt to get him to abandon his act. Almost overbalancing and toppling to the floor, Father sought to parry her efforts with his foot. I was witnessing pure farce. Regaining a vestige of composure, Father announced grandly,

"An' I'm goin' t'round off wi' one o' me favourites, 'The Swedish Rhapsody', an' I'll be playin' the last chorus of un wi' me nose!"

"Go and haul him off, quick!" snapped Rachel.

But I'd heard him perform this bright little number scores of times, he always employed it as the finale to his act, and invariably played it straight and commendably well.

"The damage is done!" I said resignedly, "We might as well let 'im do this one now, it's about the only inoffensive thing 'e knows!"

I watched as he stamped his foot and rattled out a rhythm on the tin tray with great gusto, and I quietly despaired. The last chorus reached, he raised the trusty 'gobbo' to his nose and began sniffing and snorting into it. Suddenly, the 'gobbo' fell silent. Father froze in the semi-crouched position. Both hands clutched at the instrument and the beer tray hung limply in his grasp. His eyes bulged and began to dart like those of a cornered rat. He began to tremble.

"Oh no!" I thought "The selfish bastard, a cardiac arrest on me wedding day!"

As I hastened towards him I could hear him mumbling something undecipherable. "What?" I enquired irritably.

"Da buddy dings duck do me doze!" he enunciated nasally, shooting me a panic-stricken glance.

It was stuck to his nose alright. One of the repulsive straggling hairs that hung down his nostrils like jungle creepers had somehow worked its way through the grill of the mouth organ and became inextricably trapped beneath one of the tiny metal reeds inside and as the slightest movement was making his eyes water, there was no way he could free it. Desperate situations, they say, call for desperate measures, and so, grabbing his 'gobbo' I gave it one almighty tug.

"Yaaahrgh!!!" he bellowed clutching at his throbbing nose, "You stupid bugger, you could 'ave done untold damage there!"

I looked around and smiled appeasingly at the guests, but few were keen to let their eyes meet mine. A few minutes of slack vigilance had, I felt, been my undoing.

A short while later, with most of the guests having regained at least a modicum of composure, Rachel and I prepared to leave. Aunt Cath, unfortunately, was still slumped in a chair looking decidedly brittle, as two relatives vainly attempted to revive her.

"Why dussn't burn a feather under 'er nose?" Father offered helpfully. "Allus makes the buggers sit up sharpish that does!" Thankfully he was ignored.

Rachel and I bid our farewells, and as we inched towards the door Father sidled up to me.

"I s'pose in all the excitement you've fergot 'tis me birthday t'morrer!" he mumbled with the pained expression of an unloved child.

"As a matter of fact I 'aven't!" I replied in a slightly forgiving tone "There's a card waitin' for y' on the sideboard back at Rachel's parents! 'Ere," I continued, delving deep into a trouser pocket, "'Ave this fiver an' take yerself an' Mother out somewhere t'morrow an' enjoy yourselves!"

He inspected the crumpled note with an expression of total disdain, as though I'd just tried to palm him off with a fistful of counterfeit Tunisian dinars. "Well I'm buggered!" he moaned, smacking his lips together in pointed sarcasm, "Looks like bein' a main dry day t'morrer then don't it?"

At this point the assembled Scottish contingent – minus the languishing Aunt Cath – touchingly broke into an impromptu rendition of 'Will ye no come back again?' Father spun round thinking that perhaps it was being sung for him – it wasn't.

THE END